FOR KIDS' SAKE

Winning the Tug-of-War
for Future Generations

H. B. LONDON, JR.
NEIL B. WISEMAN

Regal

From Gospel Light
Ventura, California, U.S.A.

PUBLISHED BY REGAL BOOKS
FROM GOSPEL LIGHT
VENTURA, CALIFORNIA, U.S.A.
PRINTED IN THE U.S.A.

Regal Books is a ministry of Gospel Light, a Christian publisher dedicated to serving the local church. We believe God's vision for Gospel Light is to provide church leaders with biblical, user-friendly materials that will help them evangelize, disciple and minister to children, youth and families.

It is our prayer that this Regal book will help you discover biblical truth for your own life and help you meet the needs of others. May God richly bless you.

For a free catalog of resources from Regal Books/Gospel Light, please call your Christian supplier or contact us at 1-800-4-GOSPEL *or* www.regalbooks.com.

Scripture quotations are from
THE MESSAGE—Scripture taken from *THE MESSAGE.* Copyright © by Eugene H. Peterson, 1993, 1994, 1995. Used by permission of NavPress Publishing Group.
NIV—Scripture taken from the *Holy Bible, New International Version*®. Copyright © 1973, 1978, 1984 by International Bible Society. Used by permission of Zondervan Publishing House. All rights reserved.
NKJV—Scripture taken from the *New King James Version.* Copyright © 1979, 1980, 1982 by Thomas Nelson, Inc. Used by permission. All rights reserved.

Cover and interior design by Robert Williams
Edited by Dean Rea

Library of Congress Cataloging-in-Publication Data

Wiseman, Neil B.
  For kids' sake / Neil Wiseman and H. B. London.
    p. cm.
Includes bibliographical references.
  ISBN 0-8307-3244-6
  1. Church work with children. 2. Family—Religious
aspects—Christianity. 3. Children—Religious life. I. London, H. B.
II. Title.
  BV639.C4.W57 2004
  259'.22—dc22   2003022737

1 2 3 4 5 6 7 8 9 10 11 12 13 14 15 / 09 08 07 06 05 04

Rights for publishing this book in other languages are contracted by Gospel Light Worldwide, the international nonprofit ministry of Gospel Light. Gospel Light Worldwide also provides publishing and technical assistance to international publishers dedicated to producing Sunday School and Vacation Bible School curricula and books in the languages of the world. For additional information, visit www.gospellightworldwide.org; write to Gospel Light Worldwide, P.O. Box 3875, Ventura, CA 93006; or send an e-mail to info@gospellightworldwide.org.

CONTENTS

Part 2—The Amazing Power of God's Family

Part 3—Builders of Future Generations

I WAS THERE AND FELT THE PAIN

As I spoke during a memorial service and later talked to the parents of high school students who were killed or injured during a shooting at West Paducah, Kentucky, I felt their pain.

What a waste, what an affront to all that is decent and good, what a sad commentary on the plight of our children in a society in which shootings occurred on school campuses not only in West Paducah but also in Jonesboro, Arkansas; San Diego, California; Springfield, Oregon; and Littleton, Colorado. Innocent children died, the victims of angry, abused and, in many ways, unloved classmates.

Kids have a way of pulling at the heartstrings of the world.

Remember Jessica, the little girl who was trapped in a pipe far below the surface in Midland, Texas? As rescuers worked day and night, a nation held its breath and prayed for a miracle. Millions who watched on TV were moved to the depths of their emotions as Jessica was returned safely to her parents under the glare of floodlights.

You may recall the saga of a six-year-old Cuban boy, Elian Gonzales. His mother, along with others, drowned while attempting to escape Cuba. Elian survived, and the tug-of-war over whether he was to remain in the United States or be returned to Cuba captivated the entire world. After months of wrangling, he was returned to his father in Cuba.

The kidnapping of Elizabeth Smart later dominated the media's attention for several months and then became old news until she was discovered walking down a street with her captors near Salt Lake City, Utah. Her parents, who had kept a constant vigil, called her return a miracle.

The tipping point that something had to be done by everybody came for me in Paducah, Kentucky. You remember the story. On December 1, 1997, young people arrived early for school at West Paducah and formed a prayer circle in the school foyer and prayed before school began. Watching from the perimeter was a 14-year-old boy, Michael Carneal, who for some reason was agitated and confused. As the prayer concluded, the young man began to shoot his fellow students. Three of them were killed and five others were wounded before he surrendered.

A year later, I was asked to participate in the healing service for those who suffered the pain of those senseless killings. That event will remain etched in my memory for the rest of my life.

Among those present was the mother of one of the slain girls. When I completed my remarks, she approached me, thanked me for my words of comfort and said something I will never forget.

"I guess you know, pastor, that our lives will never be the same," she said. Then she continued, "Our home is so quiet. Her life was so vibrant. Our house is so quiet now." Before I could reply, she said, "We miss her so."

I asked her how they were coping with the great loss. She thought for a moment and said, "The only way we can face the next day is in knowing that our daughter is in heaven and we will see her again one day."

Then she was distracted for a split second because she turned in the direction of a man whose back was to us. She looked back at me and said, "Do you see that man?" I nodded. "That's our pastor. If it were not for him, my daughter might never have turned her life over to the Lord. We will ever be indebted to him."

She began to weep quietly. I cried with her, and then she touched my arm and disappeared in the crowd.

As I write these words, I can still hear that heartbroken mother say to me, "I guess you know our lives will never be the same again." Thousands of people in our world could repeat her words today. I pray, however, that those will never be your words. We must, by all means, save our children.

H. B. London, Jr.

INTRODUCTION

SOUND THE ALARM AND SAVE THE CHILDREN

Like Peter before the Sanhedrin, we two pastors—H. B. and Neil—cannot help but shout in protest about what we see and hear as we travel each year to many sites of our ministry. We're morally infuriated when we see the plight of so many kids—those who are victims of divorce, of poverty, of abuse. Emotionally scarred, spiritually starved children compel us to ask significant questions about the future of our communities, country and society.

The deafening alarms sound like unstoppable thunder combined with the fury of a thousand tornadoes. Attacks of evil and pain target our children, our most precious treasure.

This war zone encompasses our homes, schools, churches, communities and hearts. The subtle and sometimes deadly weapons include our TVs and computers.

The future of civilization, the future of the Church, the future of the family and the future of a soul-satisfying way of life depend on our efforts to help children discover the magnetic attraction of Jesus. They are the Church of tomorrow as well as the Church of today.

There are many verifiable facts documenting the desperate situations our kids face. It's time to study the facts and to step up our efforts to save the new generation.

Our master said, "Bring the children to me" (see Mark 10:14, Luke 18:16). We offer suggestions for everyone who has even one child in his or her life, especially pastors and laypeople, about how to respond to this compelling need. If we meet this challenge, lives will be salvaged and the Church will be strengthened.

Those people who take a child by the hand and lead him or her to Jesus win a mother's heart, a father's gratitude and God's favor. Who knows—the hope of humanity may reside in that child's fulfilled spiritual potential.

THE FRIGHTENING FACTS

Present catastrophic changes—"Over the past several decades, dramatic changes have reshaped America's families. Young adults have delayed marriage. Cohabitation before marriage has become more commonplace. One in three women giving birth is now unmarried, up from 5 percent in 1960."[1]

Child population in the United States—"In 2000, there were 70.4 million children under age 18 in the United States, or 26 percent of the population."[2]

Marriages in the United States—"120 million now married, 4.5+ million separated, 14.5 million widowed."[3]

Single population—"The U.S. singles population, 82 million, is larger than the national population of all but 11 of the world's 192 nations."[4]

Children living at home—"46 percent of married-couple households include children under 18."[5]

Children living in poverty—"In 2000, 16 percent of children lived in families with incomes below the poverty threshold."[6]

Living Conditions for Children

Millions involved in blended families—"One out of every three Americans is now a stepparent, stepchild, stepsibling, or some other participant in a stepfamily. About half of the 60 million children under age 13 in the United States are living with one of their biological parents and that parent's current partner."[7]

Single-parent families—"Twelve million families are single-parent families; 10 million of those are single-mother families which comprise 26 percent of all family groups. Single dads run 5 percent of all family groups."[8]

Absent fathers—"In 1960, fewer than 10 million children did not live with their fathers. Today, the number is nearly 25 million. More than one-third of these children will not see their fathers at all during the course of a year."[9]

Living with single parents—"Half of all children born since 1990 will live in a single-parent home at some time during their childhoods."[10]

Living with grandparents—About 5,435,000 children, or 7.7 percent of all children in the United States, were living in homes with a grandparent in 1997, according to the Commerce Department's Census Bureau.[11]

Grandparents responsible for care—2,456,730 children live with grandparents responsible for their care.[12]

Factors That Fragment Families

Starter marriages increasing—"Divorcing before age 30 is becoming so common that it is creating a demographic phenomenon: the starter marriage. The union lasts a few years and ends before children arrive. . . . A 2001 government survey says 20 percent of divorces in first marriages now occur within five years."[13]

Starter marriages called temporary unions—"Marriage is on the verge of becoming only a temporary union."[14]

Divorce rate keeps increasing—9.8 percent or 19,400,000 adults are divorced; 43 percent is the number of marriages that break up within 15 years.[15]

United States leads the world—"The divorce rate in the United States is the highest in the world and is two to three times what it was for our parents and grandparents. Currently about half of all couples who marry divorce within seven years."[16]

Single moms—"Fifty percent of single-mom families are a result of divorce; 43 percent have never married."[17]

Cohabitation statistics—"3.8 million unmarried couples reported cohabiting, equal to 3.7 percent of all households in the United States."[18]

Cohabitation increasing drastically—"Seven percent of American adults live with an unmarried partner. The number of unmarried-couple households rose 71 percent between 1990 and 2000."[19]

Wife abuse—"One of three women experiences at least one physical assault by a partner during adulthood."[20]

Teen abuse—"An estimated one-fifth to one-third of teenagers are regularly abusing or being abused verbally, mentally, emotionally, sexually and/or physically by their partners."[21]

Cost of abuse—"The average cost of medical treatment to abused women, children and elders is about $1,630 per person annually. Businesses pay an estimated $3 billion to $5 billion a year in medical expenses and an additional $100 million in losses due to absenteeism and reduced productivity."[22]

Fatal abuse—"Seventy percent of domestic-violence fatalities occur after the woman has left her abuser."[23]

Profile of the Contemporary Church

Born again—"Thirty-nine percent of Americans describe themselves as 'a born again Christian' (2001). Two-thirds of Americans (66 percent) say they have made a personal commitment to Jesus Christ that is still important in their life today (2001)."[24]

Believers or disciples—"Three out of five (60 percent) say they are deeply spiritual. Four out of 10 adults say they are 'evangelical Christians.' 39 percent say they are 'born again Christians' (2001)."[25]

Image of Christianity—"Only one-third of those who have no connection with Christianity have a favorable impression of born-again Christians; just one-fifth feel positively toward evangelicals."[26]

Commitment reality—"Forty-one percent of adults who attend church services in a typical week are not born again."[27]

Small churches attract new believers—"One-quarter of the churched-as-children crowd affiliates with one of the nation's 340,000 Protestant or Catholic congregations that claims less than 100 adults; one-third of the unchurched-as-a-child group does so. People under 35 and women were among those most inclined to attend such congregations."[28]

Influence of religion—"Two out of three adults (66 percent) contend that religion is losing its influence in American society."[29]

Church's perceived relevance—"The Christian church is currently *not* among the top dozen influences, as it had been in the past. The leading influencers of U.S. society today are: movies, television, the Internet, books, music, public policy and law, and family."[30]

Church attendance—"Eighty-three percent of the people in the pews are regular attenders; 50 is the average age of a regular worshiper."[31]

Backyard mission field—"In 1900 we had 27 churches for every 10,000 Americans. By 1950 there were only 17 churches for every 10,000 people. Now there are fewer than 11 churches per 10,000 Americans. Some 60 to 65 million people over 18 are unchurched—one-third of the adult population."[32]

PART 1

CHILDREN:
A GENERATION
IN CRISIS

We pray for children
who are overprogrammed by school,
sports and music lessons,
who spend all their allowance before
Wednesday,who want pizza and hot dogs rather than meat and
broccoli;

and we pray for children
who were born with AIDS or HIV,
who saw Daddy make a drug deal on the
front porch last night,
who attend schools with second-rate teachers
and leaking roofs.

CHAPTER 1

CAN'T YOU HEAR THE CHILDREN CRYING?

Listen with Your Heart

Being a kid these days is tough—harder than ever before. Unthinkable tragedies and dizzying upheaval in society have scarred our children's emotions and increased their fears. Children's sense of security has turned into worrisome panic. Sensually saturated TV and hardcore Internet pornography have helped rob our kids of their innocence.

Every social evil negatively impacts children. And every frightening TV report makes children think that they could be the next victims. They are worried, frightened and some are even afraid to go outdoors or to walk to school.

Terrorists flew giant jets into the World Trade Center in Manhattan, the Pentagon in Washington, D.C., and an open field in Pennsylvania. Thousands died. The crash sites looked like the jaws of hell. The nation mourned. In some families, a parent who left for work on September 11, 2001, never came home.

Regrettably, children of all ages—perhaps most of the nation's 70 million children—had front-row seats as the tragedy was repeated endlessly on TV. No wonder child psychologist Dan Kindlon felt compelled to write how all of this would affect children:

> In the light of 9/11, I suddenly found myself, the father of two young children, caught up in a tragic historical event. The world in which my children were growing up had shifted on its axis. The rules had changed. It was no longer clear that they would always enjoy the comfort and security that most of us have.[1]

Like the flood tide of an angry river, horrible events keep coming that frighten our kids and us.

Oklahoma City's children still suffer because a madman used a truck bomb to even some score with the government. One hundred seventy-two children lost a parent. A nation mourned. Adults were frightened and outraged.

"Columbine"—the word has come to mean school shootings. After seeing all of the carnage, children wonder if their school will be next. Since the first school shooting in Moses Lake, Washington, in 1996, at least 25 more shootings have been reported in the United States. Thirty-eight students have been murdered, six teachers killed and more than 100 students wounded in these hate-filled incidents.[2]

Since the first school shooting in Moses Lake, Washington, in 1996, at least 25 more shootings have been reported in the United States.

Added to planes plowing into buildings, the Oklahoma City bombing and Columbine school shootings were many more disconcerting events. The following is a short list of national tragedies since 1996:

- Code orange security alerts
- Space shuttle *Columbia* disaster
- War with Iraq
- Washington, D.C. area snipers' wounding of a 13-year-old boy and the subsequent shutting down of school recesses and football games
- Federal agents' seizing of 6-year-old Cuban Elian Gonzalez
- Schoolyard killings in Kentucky, Oregon, Mississippi and Arkansas
- Pipe bomb exploding at the summer Olympics in Atlanta
- Paris-bound TWA flight explosion that killed 230, including a high school touring group

Every child has many reasons to be afraid for him- or herself, family and friends. The life of a child isn't easy these days.

THEY ARE ALL OUR CHILDREN, AREN'T THEY?

Former Senator Sam Nunn has told about a small girl gunned down by a sniper during the Sarajevo conflict.

At the moment of the shooting, a reporter dropped his pencil and pad as he rushed to the man who was holding the seriously wounded child and helped them into his car.

As the reporter stepped on the accelerator, racing to the hospital, the man with the bleeding child on his lap pleaded, "Hurry, my child is still breathing." A moment later, "Hurry, my child is still warm." Finally, in anguish, "Hurry, oh, my God, my child is getting cold."

When they arrived at the hospital, the girl was dead. As the two men washed blood from their hands and clothes, the man turned to the reporter and said, "This is a terrible task for me. I must go tell her father that his child is dead. He will be heartbroken."

The reporter was amazed. As he looked at the grieving man, he said with surprise, "I thought she was your child."

The man looked back and said, "No, but aren't they all our children?"[3]

He is right. They are all our children, and they are crying. Some are even dying, shooting each other and killing themselves. Such incidents worry our children, many of whom are crying for hundreds of dismal reasons. When we listen with our hearts, their sobs wound us deeply and make us want to find ways to alleviate their misery.

Some at-risk children are close by; other children are in foreign lands. Can you hear them crying? Will you do something to help the following children?

- *Refugee children* sobbing for their family in their homeland
- *Inner-city children* crying for friends who died in drive-by shootings
- *Latchkey children* wiping tears as they go home to empty houses
- *Depressed children* crying for help as they consider killing themselves
- *Rejected children* crying because they are shut out of cliques
- *Brokenhearted children* weeping because their parents have divorced

- *Frightened children* quietly weeping after being bullied by classmates
- *Juvenile killers* sobbing in prison cells because they committed adult crimes

HOW DO CHILDREN PERSONALIZE TRAGEDIES?

Like many adults, children worry about situations that are out of control or fear events that likely will never occur. Many of them think of a TV report as something very close to home. They begin expecting the worst news to come to fruition in their own lives. Think how traumatized kids feel about issues like divorce, death, drugs, peer rejection, alcohol, absentee parents, sexual abuse, suicide, AIDS, guns and career-driven parents. Innocence is being lost earlier than at any other time in history. As a child, did you have worries like these?

A 7-year-old boy in Denver told his mother as he was being tucked into bed for the night, "I am sorry to see people die. I am glad I do not have to go to that school. I'm afraid to grow up."

A 10-year-old girl told her teacher she feared being raped because of what she saw in the ghetto where she lived.

A 12-year-old boy asked his dad if they could move out of New York City to a safe place in the country.

A SWAT team police officer—one of the first to answer the call to Columbine High School and a father whose children attended that school—said that it was too up close and personal. That's what many feel these days. Littleton, Jonesboro, Springfield and Paducah are not the only places where those headlines potentially exist. Thousands of disasters are waiting to happen in many locations.

Imagine what it was like for children who lived near Ground Zero in New York. Their world was fractured in an instant. After the tragedy, one displaced boy had new clothes, new toys, went out to dinner every day for weeks and stayed in friends' apartments because the building where he had lived was no longer habitable. But that didn't ease his pain. He wanted to go home.

HOW DO WE ANSWER THE HARD QUESTIONS FOLLOWING THE TEARS?

"What are the answers?" Jefferson County (Colorado) sheriff John Stone asked following the Littleton shooting. Visibly shaken by what he saw during the investigations, his voice quivered with grief as he answered his own question, "We don't have the answers."[4]

Another civic leader said, "We must seize the moment and do something."

Everybody wants the haunting questions answered: Why do children commit violent acts? What can we do? Why do I feel so helpless?

A significant answer to this moral riddle popped up in a TV interview Tim Russert had with Janet Reno, then attorney general of the United States. Russert asked if the federal government could do anything about this school violence. Reno replied that everybody can do something about it.

Perhaps the best way to seek answers is to listen carefully to questions from ordinary people who try to sort through the problems.

Does anyone listen to children? An insightful article written by a teenager for the *Denver Post* following the Littleton shootings offered this advice to adults: "Teens want parents to hear them, and they will talk. When they do talk to you, listen and do not tell them what is right and wrong and what to think. Just listen."[5]

Are kids taught to value the right things? Mary Pipher, in her engaging foreword to William Pollack's book *Real Boys*, said, "All children are growing up in a culture in which adults are teaching them to love the wrong things."[6] It's a serious charge, but it seems true, doesn't it? This reality demands attention in a society that is overfocused on stuff, status and financial security. Many children have everything they want but little of what they need.

Does the coarsening of society contribute to the problems of children? The coarsening of society shows up in obscenities shouted in gridlock traffic. Four-letter words are often used on TV talk shows. The issue is so common in our society that Elizabeth Austin asked the question, "Can we get along without the 'F' word?"[7]

Shunned by cliques? The need for belonging is as human as bones and brains. Not being accepted by peers often makes a child feel like a worthless outcast. The problem compounds when insiders tease or when outsiders harass. At Columbine, the teen killers were considered strangely weird— members of the trench-coat mafia. Some fellow students say tormentors sometimes shoved

Many children have everything they want but little of what they need.

the perpetrators into their lockers. Such bullying invites trouble. The rage it creates can become lethal, as it did at Columbine.

Where were the parents? Stephen Carter throws a bright new light on this issue: "Parents do not act in a vacuum; they act in a culture. And the culture sends its own messages. When those messages are in competition, rather than cooperation, with what parents try to teach, we can predict trouble."[8] Parents must be continuously vigilant, frequently evaluating attitudes and actions of their children. The pressing challenge is to really know children and to become reacquainted with them as they grow from one stage to the next. Understanding a 14-year-old is different from relating to a 10-year-old.

Is self-love the problem? A Denver newspaper columnist speaks to this ever-present issue like a flaming Old Testament prophet: "We—the most self-indulgent, self-adoring, self-esteemed generation in history—have screwed it up—in our forever-adolescent vernacular—'big time.' We've indulged our kids and ourselves with unprecedented materialism. We've pursued interests and careers with unparalleled zeal while relegating our children's care and upbringing to hired substitutes, schools and government."[9] Youth coddled with self-love and surrounded by violence may be the incendiary root for what is happening these days.

Harvard psychologist Dan Kindlon agrees. After quoting then-President Jimmy Carter's assessment that Americans are beset by a malaise—a crisis of the spirit characterized by self-indulgence and consumption—Kindlon makes a strong case that self-centered values make it difficult for children to cope with adversity. He says, "Me-first attitude can compromise the health of our society when a crisis demands personal sacrifice."[10] Parents, children and church leaders alike need the quiet word of Teresa of Avila: "We shall never succeed in knowing ourselves unless we seek to know God."[11]

Has faith been lost from the soul of our society? Maybe not completely lost, but faith is distant, puny and mute. Something is radically wrong, for example, when hateful comments, class-made videos depicting killings, black trench coats and even Nazi salutes were allowed in the name of tolerance at Columbine

High School. Something is radically wrong in a society that, in the name of free speech, allows national magazines to publish endless trash about commitment-free sex for teens or a perfume company to run a line of advertisement that says, "If living with obsession is a sin, then let me be guilty!"

To such a situation, Os Guiness says, "Let them tithe their profits to contribute to the recovery and care of young lives ruined by sexual abuse. American children are not the problem. American adults are. But it is hardly fair that adults rethink the causes only when children pay the consequences."[12]

WHERE IS OUR SPIRITUAL AWAKENING?

On May 27, 1999, Darrell Scott addressed the United States House of Representatives. Scott is the father of two victims of the Columbine shootings: a daughter, Rachel Joy, who was killed, and a son, Craig, who survived.

In his blunt testimony, Scott sounded like a modern-day Jeremiah: "The death of my wonderful daughter, Rachel Joy Scott, and the deaths of that heroic teacher and the other children who died must not be in vain. Columbine was not just a tragedy. It was a spiritual event that should be forcing us to look at where the real blame lies!"[13]

The grief-stricken father courageously continued by reading a poem that should be heard by every civic leader at all levels of government. He said: "I wrote a poem four nights ago that expresses my feelings best," he said. "That was before I knew I would be speaking here today.

> "Your laws ignore our deepest needs.
> Your words are empty air.
> You've stripped away our heritage.

You've outlawed simple prayer.
Now gunshots fill our classrooms.
And precious children die.
You seek for answers everywhere.
And ask the question 'Why?'
You regulate restrictive laws
Through legislative creed.
And yet you fail to understand
That God is what we need."[14]

Then Darrell Scott somberly offered this chilling analysis: "The real villain lies within our own hearts. Political posturing and restrictive legislation are not the answers. The young people of our nation hold the key. There is a spiritual awakening taking place that will not be squelched. We do not need more religions. We do not need more gaudy television evangelists spewing out verbal religious garbage. We do not need more million-dollar church buildings built while people with basic needs are being ignored. We do need a change of heart and a humble acknowledgment that this nation was founded on the principle of simple trust in God."[15]

Denver Post columnist Ken Hamblin sounded a clear-as-day wake-up call to this moral barrenness in our national psyche: "With adolescents slaughtering one another in increased record numbers, we don't have a lot to lose by reintroducing God and the spiritual principles of right and wrong back into America's public schools."[16]

Jesus' directive to His disciples challenges us, too: "I'm telling you, once and for all, that unless you return to square one and start over like children, you're not even going to get a look at the kingdom, let alone get in. *Whoever becomes simple and elemental again, like this child, will rank high in God's kingdom.* What's more, when you receive the childlike on my account, it's the same as receiving me" (Matt. 18:3-5, *THE MESSAGE*, emphasis added).

Our Lord's priority of children is clear: Whoever welcomes a child welcomes Him. The rewards are magnificent, because no one can sincerely try to help another without being helped in return.

We pray for children
who love to play in the mud and wonder how
their clothes got dirty,
who have computers and Game Boy and
Nintendo video games,
who spill their cereal and forget to say grace;

and we pray for children
who suffer from verbal abuse every day,
who live with constant fear that divorce
will split their family,
who babysit themselves and watch TV till
Mom comes home.

CHAPTER 2

IF I WERE A KID TODAY, I'D LIVE IN A HOSTILE WORLD

Children Need a New World

Grandparents love to relate their childhood memories about the good old days, a time when they ran freely in neighborhoods, played games in unfenced backyards and walked unsupervised to and from school. The thought of locking doors or installing burglar alarm systems in homes was unheard of in many communities.

Today, we fence our yards, gate our communities and drive our kids to and from school even though we only live a block or two away. Strangers are suspect. Windows are barred. Doors are double locked. Security systems are standard in homes and vehicles.

As a small-town, rural, stable society started to disappear, faith foundations were forsaken, and family ties often were loosened, frayed or disappeared. An increasing number of marriages failed. Children became more frequent targets of violence in our streets, in our schools and in our homes.

Childhood has changed drastically since Elizabeth Akers Allen penned the poem "Rock Me to Sleep," in which she wrote:

Backward, turn backward,
Time, in your flight;
Make me a child again, just for tonight. [1]

Granted, many changes that affect children are positive. For example, children no longer suffer from diseases that once killed thousands before adulthood. Children in middle-class homes enjoy good dental care, including expensive braces for their teeth, and skilled pediatricians keep watch over their physical well-being. Public schools in many communities are blessed with adequate resources and become a significant factor in a family's decision on where to live.

Today's children live in a fascinating world of Disney, Game Boy, McDonald's, kids TV programming, videos and Toys "R" Us. Many children have their own rooms equipped with TV, phone, sound system and computer, and furniture designed for their use.

But distressing evidence soon dispels any notion that childhood is idyllic. Research proves that childhood doesn't mirror the storybook innocence of another era. To use a Martin Luther King, Jr., phrase, childhood has become a social and spiritual catastrophe.

The list of lost innocence is long. It leaves in its wake the havoc of broken and disrupted lives beset by divorce, illegitimate births, abortion, welfare-supported children, single-parent families, absentee fathers, hostility between the sexes, child abuse, serial killings, teenage suicides, wife battering, runaway children, food addictions, drugs, illicit sex, alcohol and gambling. These are not merely social problems. They are the individual life stories of the people who enter the front doors of our churches as visitors and move down the block as our neighbors.

Os Guiness is right: "Nowhere is America more inventive than in discovering new ways to destroy families."[2]

Many parents invest great effort in their children's education and dollars galore into sports and physical conditioning. Those same kids often watch hours of unsupervised TV each day, including violent and shockingly explicit sexual programs. Teens, still children themselves, give birth to another generation of children in which one in three babies is born to unmarried parents. One in three children is behind a year or more in school. And one in four children is born poor.[3]

Compassion International offers these heartbreaking facts about America's shameful neglect of her young:

- Every 9 seconds a child drops out of school.
- Every 10 seconds a child is reported abused or neglected.
- Every 15 seconds a child is arrested.
- Every 36 seconds a child is born into poverty.
- Every minute a baby is born to a teen mother.
- Every 3 minutes a child is arrested for drug abuse.
- Every 4 minutes a child is arrested for an alcohol-related offense.
- Every 23 minutes a child is wounded by gunfire.
- Every weekday juvenile crime peaks from 3 P.M. to 7 P.M., when nearly 5 million children in our country are left home alone after school.[4]

Meanwhile, millions of children today know almost nothing about the Bible or the church. Unfortunately, that fact doesn't seem to create a strong sense of urgency in the church, in the home or in society in general.

At the same time, thousands of teens and young adults who have no training or skills are without jobs and hope. Columnist Bob Herbert of *The New York Times* says, "In Chicago there are nearly 100,000 young people, ages 16 to 24, who are out of work, out of school and all but out of hope. In New York City there are more than 200,000. Nationwide, according to a new study by a team from Northeastern University in Boston, the figure is a staggering 5.5 million and growing."[5]

One 15-year-old put it this way: "All the kids I see are in a rush to grow up, and I don't blame them. I wouldn't want to be a child again."[6]

Why has the wish to "make me a kid again" become "I wouldn't want to be a child again"? The answer is not difficult to discover. Try asking yourself, *What might my life be like if I were a kid today?*

Why has the wish to "make me a kid again" become "I wouldn't want to be a child again"?

A CHILD'S HOSTILE WORLD

If I were a kid today, I would find the world increasingly hostile toward my generation.

Through centuries of human history, children have been valued as people who will carry on the family name, as contributors to family livelihood and as delights for their childlike ways. Bible verses such as Psalm 127:3,5 (*NKJV*), which states, "Children are a heritage from the LORD, . . . Happy is the man who has his quiver full of them" reflect the general attitude of society in the past toward children.

Today, such welcoming attitudes have changed. In technologically advanced societies like ours, boys and girls have largely become consumers rather than contributors. As a result, some people now regard them as liabilities. Not only are sons and daughters expensive to rear, but also to some potential parents children are serious hindrances to self-fulfillment, to being able to do "my own thing" and to being "my own person."

One childless career woman pointed out, "Without kids I have the time to see who I am, what I am, what I want and where I want to go. I never could have done this with children. I would have felt trapped." A grandfather who overheard her self-centered tirade remarked acidly, "And she would have made her children terribly messed up emotionally and spiritually."[7]

Yes, if I were a kid today, I would encounter a world that is becoming increasingly unfriendly to children.

A HOSTILE WORLD OF FAMILY DYSFUNCTION

If I were a kid today, I would likely have to face one or more issues stemming from family dysfunction.

In 1970, the United States Bureau of the Census conducted a study, "America's Children at Risk," and followed it up with data from the 1996 population survey. The study is helpful for understanding five risks related to the American family:

1. *Poverty.* During 1995, 21 percent of American children under age 18 lived in families below the poverty level as compared with only 15 percent in 1970.
2. *Absentee parents.* In 1996, 4 percent of children lived with neither parent, up from 3 percent in 1970. The number of children living with grandparents, with neither parent present, jumped from fewer than 1 million in 1990 to 1.4 million in 1996.

3. *One-parent families.* In 1996, 28 percent of children lived in one-parent families, more than double the 12 percent in 1970.

4. *Unwed mothers.* In 1996, 9 percent of children lived with never-married mothers compared with fewer than 1 percent in 1970.

5. *Uneducated parents.* In 1996, 19 percent of children lived with a parent or guardian who had not graduated from high school as compared with 38 percent in 1970.[8]

Another issue is divorce. Elizabeth Kolbert, a regular contributor to *The New York Times*, summarizes our present situation: "Divorce, longevity and deferred childbearing have all rendered what is now being called the 'traditional family'—mom, dad and their biological progeny—increasingly exceptional. Fully a quarter of the children born in the decade of the '90s are being raised by single parents, and there are now more American households composed of people living alone and more households of childless couples than there are households consisting of married parents living with children. Since 1970, the proportion of 'traditional' families has fallen by 35 percent."[9]

Due to these ever-increasing issues of divorce, some children are always angry toward one or both parents and worry continuously about the future. While expert opinion for many years seemed to say that divorce is not the end of the world for children, some social scientists suggested it might even be good for some. Meanwhile, children were writing heartbreaking letters to their favorite authors, seeking help and sharing their panic. "My parents are divorced," one child wrote. "My dad is the kind of person who never wants to be around kids." In another letter, a girl confides, "I wish I could sue my parents for malpractice, but I know I can't so I just try to forget what they do."[10]

When God designed families, He planned that parents would provide their children with love and security, protection, moral and spiritual instruction, discipline and emotional support in time of crisis. To reenergize the teaching of these values, the church must help mend failing marriages by saying, "If your marriage is stale, crippled or boring, fix it rather than junk it." It's time for the people of God to get as excited about saving troubled marriages as they are about weddings. In any event, rejuvenating a sick marriage usually takes much less effort than getting a divorce or remarrying.

Divorce, more than any other condition in society, leaves children defenseless in a frightening world where boundaries are fuzzy, where relationships are distorted and where security has been seriously compromised. If I were a kid today, I would worry about other friends at church and school

It's time for the people of God to get as excited about saving troubled marriages as they are about weddings.

who have seen their families fall apart and are trying to cope with the results. And even if my home appears stable, I might wonder whether divorce might someday destroy my family.

A HOSTILE WORLD OF ABUSE

If I were a kid today, those people who are closest to me—namely, my parents or a relative—might physically, emotionally or sexually abuse me.

The United States Department of Justice reports, "In 1998 there were an estimated 903,000 victims of child maltreatment nationwide. The rate of 12.9 per 1,000 children decreased from 13.7 per 1,000 children in 1997. . . . An estimated 1,100 children died of abuse and neglect, a rate of approximately 1.6 per 100,000 children in the general population."[11]

The report continues and sounds rather clinical until we realize these statistics represent children like Tom or Eric or Pablo or Patrick, kids on your street and even in your church.

Each year over 3 million children are reported victims of physical, sexual, verbal and emotional abuse; neglect; abandonment and death—and those are only the ones that were reported. In the year 2000 approximately 5 million reports were made. Of those 5 million-plus kids, over 98,000 children were treated just for sexual abuse.[12]

Child abuse is reported on average of once every 10 seconds. Because so many cases of child abuse go unreported, it is estimated that three times the number reported are actual child abuse victims. Each year almost 1.8 million children are reported missing, many of them abducted from their own homes and front yards.[13]

In the United States, children are more apt to die from abuse than from accidents. Child abuse permanently disables 18,000 children and youth every year and 565,000 are seriously injured every year.[14]

A HOSTILE WORLD OF VIOLENCE

If I were a kid today, I would live in a world of violence and fear.

Several years ago, a Hyde Park bank in the greater Chicago area sponsored a children's writing contest called My Neighborhood. The bank expected to receive a whimsical view of Chicago from the perspective of children. Surprisingly, the bank received stacks of essays and poems from frightened kids.

Consider their fears:

- An 8-year-old boy titled his essay "Trapped in My House." He wrote, "I only go outside when I get in the car or go to school. I don't like my neighborhood because they shoot too much. They might shoot me, so I stay inside."
- A 10-year-old boy wrote a six-sentence essay, including this sentence: "People get killed by shooting mostly every night."
- Eleven-year-old Cynthia wrote, "We cry, we weep, we can't go outside and play because our parents believe we may be killed that day."
- A fifth-grade boy from the Raymond School wrote, "My neighborhood is like a jail. I am scared to go out because you are threatened that you will get beat up. And if you tell anybody you and the person you tell are going to get shot."
- A 13-year-old wrote, "As you might know, I live in a slum. Some people call it hell on Earth and so do I."[15]

Then there is the problem of child-against-child violence. How can anyone forget the story of 5-year-old Eric, who was dropped from the fourteenth floor of a public assistance apartment complex in Chicago by two other children, ages 10 and 11? The motive: The 5-year-old refused to steal candy for the older children.[16]

Another kind of violence—girl-on-girl—is growing: "Violent girl-on-girl bullying has increased by 48 percent in just five years, according to a charity, which also warned of a rise in bullying of younger children and of alarming numbers of children attempting suicide as a result of victimization." [17]

Of course, all children do not live in such violent surroundings, but too many do. Many kids fear for their lives every day. And some of those fearful children live in your community and perhaps attend your church.

A HOSTILE WORLD OF TELEVISION ADDICTION

If I were a kid today, my closest friend might be my television set.

Why do children spend so much time watching TV? In many homes, the people on TV are the only people in the house for long periods of time.

Author Kate Moody, in her book *Growing Up on Television*, wrote, "The typical child sits in front of the television about four hours a day—and for children in lower socioeconomic families the amount of viewing is even greater. In either case, the child spends more time with TV than he or she spends talking to parents, playing with peers, attending school or reading books. TV time usurps family, play time and the reading time that could promote language development."[18]

What kind of friend do kids have in television? A friend who inhibits social development, wastes intellectual potential, presents an inaccurate view of faith, normalizes violence, sells secular values and saturates the mind with non-Christian worldviews.

A HOSTILE WORLD OF SCHOOL PROBLEMS

If I were a kid today, I would live in a world of troubled schools.

Many American schools need to pay more attention to providing every child a quality education and less attention to the latest faddish theories about self-discovery. While Johnny and

Annie still can't read or write, decision makers are mired in states' rights, cutthroat funding competition, athletic priorities and nonacademic social issues. Meanwhile, many high school graduates are not literate enough to complete job application forms much less perform efficiently on a job or to enter college. And in many schools, teachers say they are unable to persuade parents to return notes or to attend parent-teacher conferences.

Other problems show up at school, too. In a recent year, 47 violent deaths took place in American public schools—38 were homicides, 6 were suicides, 2 involved suspects killed by a law enforcement officer in the line of duty and 1 was unintentional. In 2000, 128,000 children ages 12 to 18 were victims of serious violent crimes at school. And in 2001, 8 percent of the students reported they had been bullied at school at least once during the year.[19]

A HOSTILE WORLD OF INSECURE PARENTS

If I were a kid today, I would live in a world where young people manipulate parents to make them feel guilty.

In a society where working parents have limited time for children, in a world where designer clothes and expensive athletic shoes top the list of artificial needs and in a culture where cash registers at toy stores ring up sales nearly as fast as the grocery markets, some family specialists believe that children set the priorities for family choices about churches, vacations, cars and fast foods.

Pastor Roger Thompson preached an intriguing sermon titled "Kids Rule," in which he warned, "I wonder if we realize the massive shift that has taken place in the last 40 years in this country? Do we understand how deeply we've been affected by the secular view of children? The bottom line is this: Kids rule and don't you question it." He cautioned later in the same message, "Don't dare touch the educational philosophy of our land, which says that children are on the throne. Parents line up; kids rule. Their wishes, their feelings, their happiness reign supreme."[20]

Children from affluent homes are sometimes thought not to be at risk, but they are. Too often parents buy their kids everything and fail to help them believe anything. Harvard psychologist Robert Coles, a specialist in faith formation for children, brings these issues into crystal-clear focus:

> For 15 to 20 years now, when I have asked American people what they believe in, they have said, "I believe in my children." Now when children have become a source of almost idolatrous, religious faith that is quite a burden for children to bear. Parents forget that what children really need perhaps more than anything else is discipline and a sense of commitment to something larger than themselves.[21]

A HOSTILE WORLD OF FEELING UNWANTED AT CHURCH

If I were a kid today, I would live in a world where I don't always feel wanted at church.

Two thousand years ago, Jesus said, "Let the little children come to Me, and do not forbid them; for of such is the kingdom of God" (Mark 10:14, *NKJV*). How well are we carrying out His directive for serving children?

There are disturbing signs indicating how some churches view children. For example, a children's pastor was asked to take charge of a series of children's services at a neighboring church to be held simultaneously with adult services. When the pastor asked what kind of program the church preferred, the answer was, "We don't care what you do with them as long as you keep them out of the adult service."

A harried children's leader in another church said the most persistent problem is trying to find children's workers. Week after week, he places notices in the church newsletter, begging people to help with Sunday School, children's church and week-day scouting. Week after week he receives a succession of no responses or resignations of people who say, "I don't want to miss regular worship services to serve children" or "I've worked with children long enough."

A national denominational leader of children's ministries tells about a letter from a woman who was heartbroken because the church decision group did not want boys and girls she was bringing on a bus to attend some church social functions. The reason: "They're too noisy and they don't know how to behave." So, the teacher wrote for guidance on how to tell the children they were not welcome.

That same children's specialist remarked in frustration, "I see churches where the rooms for children are the shabbiest in the building. I see others where the rooms are beautifully paint-ed and carpeted, but where teachers have been informed they are not to fasten anything to the walls for fear of marring the paint. I see churches where one frazzled worker struggles to teach a group of 25 to 30 kindergartners, a class nearly three times the size recommended for effective teaching. I see churches where virtually no outreach to children is being made outside the exist-ing adult membership. I see churches that find adequate funds for every concern except children. When I see such things, I real-ize that even in today's church a child might not feel welcome."[22]

Could it be that some churches allow secular cultural views of the next generation to color their attitudes toward children?

The secular view: "Children cost a lot of money and bring us no immediate return on our investment." How often has the church said, "We want adults because they can pay their way"?

The secular view: "Caring for children requires time, energy and self-sacrifice." "We don't want to make these sacrifices, so we don't want them." "Teaching children is too much work."

The secular view: "Children are a block to my self-fulfillment." In church, we sometimes say, "I can't work with children because I'll miss out on the other things in the church."

A psychologist once commented to Vance Packard, author of *Our Endangered Children: Growing Up in a Changing World,* "You can't do your own thing, search for your identity and raise children at the same time."[23] Applying that idea to children and the church, we might conclude:

- You can't live a careless spiritual life and be a model of Christ for children.
- You can't think only of yourself and follow Christ's command to care for children spiritually and emotionally.
- You can't be guaranteed you will have a church tomorrow if you fail to minister to children today.

If we want a family of faith in the next generation and if we want people wonderfully centered on Christ, we must win the children.

THE NEW WORLD EVERY CHILD NEEDS

Children live in a world that has become increasingly secularized and sinful. The moral direction points downhill at a faster and faster pace. Their world has shrunk to the superficial, the mediocre, the relative.

Meanwhile, the people of God—sometimes called the colony of heaven—can provide children a series of relationships that are solidly scriptural, Christ-centered spiritually and special because God is close by.

The world for too many kids has shrunk to all Earth and no eternity. Their world is family, if they have one, without faith. They live in a culture without Christ, a society without a soul. Many live in environments that can never offer them a chance to live a meaningful life.

The world for too many kids has shrunk to all Earth and no eternity.

The solution is for churches to offer unconditional acceptance, new beginnings, inner stability and emotional wholeness.

So, let's do it.

The benefits for children will be amazing and wonderful. The effort of providing such a safe, attractive place for kids will make the church great in grace and much stronger than it has ever been before in fulfilling its reason for being.

We pray for children
who have a new ball glove, the latest Schwinn bicycle
and a Razor scooter,
who wish school would self-destruct before
Tuesday's spelling test,
who say it's not fair that meat and salad come
before ice cream;

and we pray for children
who are bullied every day on their way home from school,
whose kitchen cupboard is empty,
who drop out of school to live in poverty for a lifetime.

CHAPTER 3

THE KUDZU
PARABLE

Nobody Intended Society to
Be Like It Is

Kudzu, a fast-growing lush vine, started out as an innocent, beautiful, flowering plant in a garden sponsored by the Japanese government to help celebrate the United States Centennial Exposition in Philadelphia, Pennsylvania, in 1876. It immediately became a botanical hit. Kudzu's sweet-smelling flowers and lush leaves attracted gardeners. Entrepreneurs soon tried to feed kudzu to livestock. The federal soil conservation service used kudzu to control soil erosion during the Great Depression. And in the 1940s, farmers were paid as much as $8 an acre to plant kudzu.

Today, what once was lovely and desirable has become a nuisance and an economic threat.

Kudzu grows profusely wild in the southeastern United States. Growing as much as a foot a day or 60 feet in a season, it now covers more than 7 million acres. One scientist toiled for 18 years to discover a kudzu killer. To his dismay, most herbicides failed, and one actually made kudzu grow faster. To those people who want to get rid of the plant in their yard or on their farm, it is recommended that strong weed killer be used for up to four years. Even then, some kudzu plants have been known to survive every kind of herbicide for more than 10 years.

The problem is that kudzu grows too well. Wherever it is planted, it soon takes on a life of its own, choking trees, climbing power poles and putting other plants at risk by overly shading them from the sun. It has become such a menace that the United States Department of Agriculture declared kudzu a weed in 1972.

Meanwhile, a moral kudzu has developed in the name of freedom, tolerance and modernity, which affects every child in the Western world. What started out to be well-intended legislation, law or good practice turned into another kudzu of the soul. It happens in churches, too.

THE KUDZU OF ME-ISM

Years ago, individualism started on a high plane, emphasizing the worth of every individual and the American dream of making it big. At the start, it proclaimed that everyone had equal rights and equal opportunity. The value of the individual was of utmost importance.

Somehow that idea became grossly overstated and even perverted. Today, children receive a subtle message from many sources that makes them believe they must put self first and ask of every relationship, "What is in it for me?" One critic said, "We harm children when stroking their ego has replaced stretching their minds."[1]

Individualism has become king in our culture. While we enjoy denying that we have to be first and the best, our conduct sends a much different message to our kids. Always the challenge before us is demonstrating by our actions and attitudes some equilibrium between what we say and what we do for our children.

Garrison Keillor, whom someone jokingly called one of the country's armchair theologians, gives us a down-home sense of balance of who we are and what God has done for us: "Before the world was made, when it was only darkness and mist and waters, God was well aware of Lake Wobegon, my family, our house, and He had me all sketched out down to what size my feet would be (big), which bike I would ride (a Schwinn) and the five ears of corn I'd eat for supper that night."[2]

God knows who we are and where we are, and much of who we are is what He has created us to be.

The apostle Paul enjoyed prescribing the following remedy to a society dedicated to self-seeking and selfishness: "[God] decided from the outset to shape the lives of those who love him along

Being made in the image of Jesus is immeasurably better than any self-actualization anyone could possibly imagine or plan.

the same lines as the life of his Son. The Son stands first in the line of humanity he restored. We see the original and intended shape of our lives there in him" (Rom. 8:29, *THE MESSAGE*).

Being made in the image of Jesus is immeasurably better than any self-actualization anyone could possibly imagine or plan. And teaching children this truth is a wonderfully Christ-centered way to help them reach their full potential.

THE KUDZU OF IGNORING
THE SERIOUSNESS OF SIN

Newspaper articles and TV newscasters regularly warn us of damage to the ozone layer, against trashing lakes and forests and of the possible extinction of certain animal species. Warnings are printed on cigarette wrappers, beer and wine labels and food packages. Yet the admonitions of Scripture to flee from the wrath to come (see Eph. 5:5-7), to seek forgiveness for accountable wrongs before God (see Matt. 6:12-15) and to keep the commandments (see Eccles. 12:13) are considered irrelevant.

C. S. Lewis addressed such self-defeating idiocy with candor when he said that every age has its characteristic illusions that "are likeliest to lurk in those widespread assumptions which are so ingrained in the age that no one dares to attack or feel it necessary to defend them."[3]

Even though sin is not taken seriously in our culture, it is behind every heartbreak, every injustice and every war. Every problem every child faces is either directly or indirectly the result of sin. Ignoring sin is a little like ignoring the law of gravity. It does its damage whether we acknowledge it or not. Scripture is clear about sin's seriousness when it says, "Christ died for our sins according to the Scriptures" (1 Cor. 15:3, *NIV*).

THE KUDZU OF COMPULSIVENESS

Like the lovely vine that arrived in North America in 1876, our attempts to excel and succeed are fine, even admirable unless they dominate and consume our lives. We think that as soon as we accomplish something things will be different. Or as soon as we move to a new house or can get a few days off work, life will be better. Ironically, life never gets any better—perhaps only busier, as we pursue a kudzu agenda.

Images of the good life sometimes trick us into a lifelong acquisition trap, irrationally accumulating things we don't use, don't need and eventually don't want. Think of the people who work all week to earn enough money to spend at the mall on their day off and repeat the process week after week. And what about the children in their lives, in their churches and in their neighborhoods that need them now?

Children need our devotion today as much as they will ever need us tomorrow. To paraphrase Benjamin Franklin's wise advice: Do not squander the time you could spend with a child for that is what joy and satisfaction are made of.[4]

Images of the good life sometimes trick us into a lifelong acquisition trap, irrationally accumulating things we don't use, don't need and eventually don't want.

THE KUDZU OF CONSUMERISM

It starts so subtly. We think about college educations and wedding costs on the day following the sonogram that tells us the gender of our child. Of course, this do-better-by-them idea makes us work longer hours and move to better neighborhoods. In the process, strain is placed on the marriage. Family breakdown frequently follows.

What started out to be the ideal family is overtaken by the kudzu of consumerism. More is never enough, and we settle for average marriages and dutiful parenting. Soon the costs and keeping up with the neighbors weigh us down and our primary relations at home are damaged or are sometimes destroyed.

THE KUDZU OF SCHOOLS AS SOCIAL CHANGE AGENTS

Public schools often are used to implement public policy as much as learning. Schools are committing "fraud by promising a real education and delivering something much different."[5]

At a time when schools seem to be doing so poorly—with more than 30 percent of college freshmen needing remedial courses[6]— society is entering an era where higher levels of education will be needed for competing in a service-oriented, information-driven society. Meanwhile, the general public and corporate leaders are asking tough questions about investing in a product that is failing to meet its objectives. What a collision course.

The citizenry also does strange things to compound the problem. One school district, while trying to merge two high schools to improve academics and finances, was opposed by people in the community because they didn't want to lose their football team, its colors or familiar team name.

How long can society endure declining education, vanishing families and disposable fathers? Does it not follow that children of poorly educated, never-married parents will likely become unwed parents themselves, causing our present family disasters to multiply in the coming generations?

Amazingly, when it comes to the crisis in education, many thinking people seem to be charmed into a pseudosophisticated silence.

THE KUDZU OF ROOTLESSNESS

Much like the creeping kudzu plant, Americans' pride of independence, their sense of adventure in moving up the ladder of success every three or four years and their willingness to settle hundreds or even thousands of miles away from extended families have taken a high toll on our relatedness.

This reality is described by John Steinbeck in his book *Travels with Charley*, as "a burning desire to go, to move, to get under way, anyplace from here. They spoke quietly of how they wanted to go someday, to move about, free and unanchored, not toward something but away from something."[7]

It all seems so good—the newness, the mobility, the thrill of starting over, the quick divorce, westward expansion—until our hyperactivity wears us down and we are forced to look inside ourselves.

Even the most independent person among us has a surprising dependency on feeling needed, loved and accepted.

To be human is to have a need for belonging and meaning. As the theme song from the TV program *Cheers* put it, "You want to go where everybody knows your name." Os Guiness summarized the issue: "With heaven evacuated, history severed, families strung out if not disintegrating, and faith unreal, homelessness has become an increasing menace to modern Americans."[8]

This kind of homelessness—much more than not having a

bed to sleep in or a house to live in—reaches into all economic levels of society and every generation. In short, a widespread hunger for what home represents has created a soul-deep sense of isolation.

Though the results may not be very visible, rootlessness to the human spirit is a lot like the roses from last week's wedding bouquet: a wilted reminder of what was but not much help for what is or what is to be. Even the most independent person among us has a surprising dependency on feeling needed, loved and accepted. That is especially true for children, who need roots.

Our need for a sense of belonging and relational roots is what Robert Finch described: "True belonging is born of relationships not only to one another but to a place of shared responsibilities and benefits. We love not so much what we have acquired as what we have made and whom we have made it with."[9]

THE KUDZU OF FEARING RADICAL TRANSFORMATION

We much prefer a gradual change that threatens no one, especially us. We know the family needs major overhaul, but we treat symptoms rather than the disease. Therefore, we constantly make inconsequential changes. Medical pioneer Dr. Lee Salk believes we are ready as a nation to go back to "a time when values were strong, when people were polite and respectful to one another, when spending time together and with our children was a cherished priority, when we were not desensitized to vulgar language, graffiti, intrusive noise, mounds of trash and casual violence."[10]

But is this possible without the inner miracle of conversion in individual hearts?

THE KUDZU OF DIVORCE

The kudzu divorce factor has brought us to a time "when as many as one-third of today's children will experience their parents' divorce and close to one-half will spend some time in a single-parent family before the age of 18."[11]

Angela Elwell Hunt, in an article entitled "What Children of Divorce Really Think," listed statements of children whose parents had been divorced:

- I just can't tell you how alone I feel.
- I wonder if my mom and dad ever really loved each other.
- I don't know why my mom and dad ever got married.
- I used to think I was adopted because there was no way they could have stopped fighting long enough to have me.
- I think it was my fault because I heard Mom and Dad fighting over me.
- Mom and dad expect me to "adjust," but the home I once knew is gone.
- Sometimes I'm relieved my parents are divorced. Shouldn't I want them to be together?
- My parents divorced, so I'll never get married.
- More than anything, I want my mom and dad to get together again.[12]

THE KUDZU OF FREE SPEECH

Virtue and freedom were closely tied together in the thinking of the founders of our nation. The connection is obvious as a person studies their lives and their commitments to faith and justice. What started as a great virtue and a glorious right for all people has gradually tilted, pushing freedom as far as possible without regard for consequences to the culture or responsibility to our kids.

Recently a woman, using a cell phone while standing on the sidewalk outside a doctor's office, was using language that would embarrass most sailors at sea. When asked to stop polluting the morning with her vulgarities, she said, "I have a right to say anything I want to anytime and anywhere."

When carried to its limit, freedom means a person can say or do anything at any time. But should a person not consider the consequences of his or her unfettered expression?

THE KUDZU OF HAPPINESS AT ANY COST

Happiness and satisfaction are by-products of living a life of love in service to others. But we get it all mixed up in our society—generosity turns to selfishness, faith turns to pessimism, joy turns to cynicism. Although we may not admit to being bored or unhappy, we are. And the children in our lives feel that spirit. Like kudzu, our quest for happiness starts out with the highest motives and commitments, but something sad transpires before noonday. We forget the assuring words of Psalm 16:11 (*NKJV*): "In Your presence is fullness of joy; at Your right hand are pleasures forevermore."

THE KUDZU OF LOST NEIGHBORS AND EXTENDED FAMILIES

Let me tell you about the neighborhood where I (Neil) grew up. I was reared in a close-knit neighborhood in Detroit—the community was really a metropolitan village. We were real neighbors and friendly helpers to one another. Illnesses, family crises and deaths brought outpourings of help and authentic caring.

The Buzenskis, Stubblefields, Kazakas, Greens, Blondells, Coffees, Berrys, Pickles, Binkleys, Alversons and Nichols lived on our block. I could visit them anytime, and they sometimes offered me a cold drink or a snack. They paid me for mowing their grass in the summer and for shoveling the snow from their walks in the winter. The postal carrier and the police officers were our friends. We kids played Kick-the-Can in the street because there wasn't much traffic, and we played Hide-and-Seek at dusk. Before TV and air-conditioning, neighbors visited on their front porches, and we often stopped on our walks to or from church to admire a neighbor's flowers, to ask about the grown children or to give Mr. Berry a break from caring for his wife who, if she lived today, would be cared for in a nursing home or hospice.

But like any village, our neighborhood had significant limitations. The neighborhood, however broadly defined, cannot provide everything a child needs. After the snacks at neighbors' houses, I always went home to eat regular meals. Someone at home read to me. Someone at home taught me respect for others. Someone at home insisted I share family responsibilities. Someone at home taught me to pray. Some things the neighbors just can't do for a child.

As wonderful as our neighborhood was, it wasn't the same as home. Home was more personal, more intense, more accountable, more lasting and more loving than my neighborhood. At home I belonged.

Oh, how I belonged. By birth, by name, by relationship, I was part of the fabric of home. I was perpetual and not occasional. As good as they were, neighbors were never family or blood or relatives or kin. The family nourished me, knew me from my birth, took responsibility for me and belonged to me. Those family strengths, missing in so many families today, can be experienced in our churches if we intentionally build them into the church's service to children.

TEAR DOWN THE KUDZUS

Kids need our help in eradicating the kudzus that tangle and threaten their lives. With God's help, we can cut away the clutter in our homes, in our schools, in our community and in our church. The task, however, begins with each one of us, especially with those who embrace Christ as Savior, leaning on Him for wisdom and a blueprint for change in a world that increasingly belittles the value of children.

I love to take renewed inspiration from George Bernard Shaw's words from *Man and Superman*:

> This is the true joy in life, the being used for a purpose recognized by yourself as a mighty one; the being a force of nature instead of a feverish, selfish little clod of ailments and grievances complaining that the world will not devote itself to making you happy.[13]

We pray for children
who melt our hearts with one little kiss,
who tell family secrets and feel anxious about Santa Claus,
who won't clean their rooms without a fuss;

and we pray for children
who will never go to Walt Disney World,
who have no uncles, aunts or grandparents to spoil them,
who have been molested by their priests or ministers.

CHAPTER 4

SOUL STRETCHING FOR CONTEMPORARY CHURCHES

Kids Need the Church to Live Out Its Reason for Being

Soon after the Columbine High School massacre, Oprah Winfrey, during a TV interview, asked attorney Jerry Spence, "Do we need more gun control?"

"We need more heart control," was Spence's surprising reply.[1]

Heart control. Doesn't that sound like the church's specialty?

A veteran pastor understood our present dilemma when he preached, "The heart of the matter is a matter of the heart." And Jeremiah, the prophet who lived thousands of years earlier, agreed, "The heart is deceitful above all things, and desperately wicked; who can know it?" (Jer. 17:9, *NKJV*).

Radical transformation of the soul—trading old hearts and lives for new ones—is the reason the church exists. God has placed churches in the world to help people find forgiveness of sin and to mend broken lives. It is the church's main business—

and it is much more important than building bigger buildings or fighting worship wars.

To help parents and society better interact with and react to children, the church must specialize in soul issues. The church must do its part to see that morality and values are placed much closer to the top of the public agenda. The church must loving-ly lead society to weave God's guidance and resources into the fabric of the community and of home life.

Commentator David Gergen, a best-selling author and presidential adviser, made this sobering statement: "America does have a serious problem, but it's not the younger gener-ation. We have a culture that leaves many people feeling estranged, their dignity destroyed, and this can lead to extreme antisocial behavior by those who can't find solace in their friends or family."[2]

Then Gergen offers this surprising observation: "It's time to see our kids for who they truly are. Most of them are not rude, wild and irresponsible; in fact, most of them could one day make this country an immensely better place. But all of them still need a caring, compassionate adult in daily life, helping them grow up to become all they can be."[3]

THE CHURCH IS A MYSTERY, A MIRACLE AND IS HUMAN

"Church"—many of us cannot utter the word without feeling a sense of soaring affection. The church is our spiritual home, a comfortable, secure connection, a setting where God gives meaning to our lives. The purpose given to the church by Jesus is about new beginnings, meaning, belonging and wholeness, which make it possible for every congregation to be a living cell of the everlasting Church.

The Church Is a Lofty Ideal for Paul
The apostle Paul described the Church with affectionate, powerful words: "saints" (Rom. 1:7, *NIV*), "brethren" (Romans 1:13, *NKJV*), "believers" (1 Cor. 6:5, *NIV*), "body of Christ" (1 Cor. 12:27, *NIV*) and "God's building" (1 Cor. 3:9, *NIV*).

When all of these titles are considered, it becomes obvious that Paul wanted us to realize that we are part of the living and loving Church God is building. Fellow believers are so durable and so closely connected that they are like stones forming a magnificent cathedral. The apostle knew that believers are to be a company of disciples who live in such a close relationship with Jesus that their relationship is similar to a marriage bond.

In the center of Paul's comparison between marriage and Church, as if all the metaphors he could think of were not strong enough, he added: "This is a huge mystery, and I don't pretend to understand it all" (Eph. 5:32, *THE MESSAGE*). Some commentators believe "mystery" refers to marriage. Others suggest that it refers to the Church. It could, of course, refer to both.

Every married person knows marriage is a mystery, a miracle and a human connection. Who can explain how a man and a woman, who are so different physically and emotionally, can build a happy marriage? And what married person will not say that while marriage is mystery and miracle, it also has the most human elements of all relationships?

The Church Is a Mystery
This mystery transcends rational explanation. It is God giving His people a family: a place to belong and a place to go for worship, nurturing and direction. Think of the mysteries that make the Church what it is:

- *Mystery of beginnings.* Those who made up the Early Church had limited understanding of what the Church was to be.

- *Mystery of membership.* Check the key members of the Church at Pentecost and those who made up the core group at Philippi and you have a mystery.
- *Mystery of leadership.* Early Church leaders in Jerusalem were fairly weak or inadequate, but still the Church flourished.
- *Mystery of continuance.* The Church has endured for generations. Who can explain why?
- *Mystery of Jesus' attraction.* Consider how many millions of people have aligned themselves with the Church across two millenia because they were attracted to Jesus, who always brings believers to the Cross.
- *Mystery of focus.* Throughout Christian history, the Church has tried to find a balance among redemption, purity and compassion. Even though some leaders in every generation failed to see what God was trying to do, renewal movements have brought the Church back to a New Testament focus.
- *Mystery of minority.* The Church of Jesus Christ has had powerful influence across 2,000 years even though it has always been a minority religion in almost every location.

The Church Is Divine

The divine side of the Church calls us to selfless servanthood in Jesus' name. The divine dimension fascinates and energizes our service in Christ and supplies the reason for why we commit our lives to the Church.

If we are to save the children, the supernatural dimension of the church must be rekindled, retooled, reenergized and perhaps reinvented. In other words, the church must recover its reason for being.

We must be committed to use all the riches of the Christian faith in ministry to impact the present culture. It means living the Christian faith while recognizing the uniqueness of our time in human history. The greatest Christian influencers in every generation are those who know God and know their times so well that they can apply spiritual resources to meet the needs of their generation.

Many years ago, Elton Trueblood, the authentic Christian Quaker philosopher, wrote, "There is no possibility of renewal unless we are always living on the spiritual frontier."[4]

The Church from beginning to end is all about Jesus:

Jesus is the magnetic attraction of the Church in every age and generation, including this one.

His message, His way of living, His transforming impact on us and on the world. He owns the Church. He loves the Church. He energizes the Church. He is the magnetic attraction of the Church in every age and generation, including this one.

The Church Is Human

The church's human side is among our greatest frustrations. Its wobbling, patronizing side is often weak, blind, cowardly and sometimes wickedly unfair. To its human side, three questions must be raised:

1. When did sleepy Rip Van Winkle become our hero?
2. How could a church be willing to miss its greatest

opportunities because some spiritually nearsighted lay or clergy members wish to control the uncontrollable?

3. Why do the status quo and tradition have such a death grip on the people of God?

The human side of the church needs correction, creativity, imagination and redemptive change. To meet the needs of contemporary children, the church must constantly change to meet the needs of its people while remaining the same in truth. The wisdom we need is to know what to change and what to retain.

THE VILLAGES WON'T RETURN

During a drive from Kansas City, Missouri, to Denver, Colorado, I (Neil) realized that the small towns along the way were growing smaller. In a Dairy Queen I asked people questions about their town. They told me that the population was declining along with the number of farms. Meanwhile, the size of farms was increasing because agricultural conglomerates were buying the land.

We all know that young people continue to leave small towns soon after they graduate from high school, sometimes to attend college, sometimes to enter the work force, but they move often many miles from home. As a result, they may lose a sense of "home" in their new environments.

The church now faces the task of augmenting a sense of accountability and belonging, formerly functions of family, school and community. While some people are concerned that our society will surrender the former village role to the government, it does not have the resources to replace the village and perhaps isn't even willing to try.

This scenario places a much heavier responsibility on the church, not the Church institutionally or the Church theoretically, but your church and your part in it. It requires meeting the increasing and pressing needs of children that the church has always carried plus the newer challenges that the family, school and community have abandoned.

In discussing the need for more attention being given to children, syndicated columnist William Raspberry tells of a couple who went to a restaurant to recapture an enchanting evening from their past. Years have passed and many discouraging events have taken place, but they believe the restaurant can bring back the feeling. They go to the restaurant, but the former enchantment fails to materialize. Eventually, the couple realizes the enchantment of the past was the relationship and not the restaurant.[5]

Renewing and reinventing ministry to children is like that. It is not the old strategy or the old place as much as it is the old commitment to kids.

THE CHURCH'S SOUL NEEDS STRETCHING

The stretch for the church is a long one, but a good one. Like all good exercise, the church will be stronger for the effort. And the effort will help the church refocus on determining its most pressing tasks, its highest joys and what it does best.

It is time for the church to give serious attention to reinventing itself. Researcher George Barna's strong statement must be thoughtfully and thoroughly considered: "The church must reinvent itself at the same pace our culture does (every three to five years) in order to keep up with those who are seeking spiritual direction."[6]

In an insightful article challenging the contemporary church to reinvent itself, Rob Wilkens offers these guidelines for innovation and change:

- Give careful attention to the kind of church you want to become.
- Plan to move people to spiritual growth.
- Build on the vision of Christ for His church.
- Understand (the church) as a union of divine empowerment and human effort.
- Evaluate and measure results against what Christ wants His church to be.[7]

To facilitate this vigorously stamina-strengthening endeavor, a church must work through several solvable dilemmas that tend to keep many congregations in a safe harbor when the action is out in the deep.

Apostasy: Churches Lose Their Mooring

The landscape of American Christianity is dotted with churches that have lost their reason for being. These churches typically have little or no interest in kids. Of such a church, Scripture offers this sad evaluation: "I know you inside and out, and find little to my liking. You're not cold, you're not hot—far better to be either cold or hot! You're stale. You're stagnant. You make me want to vomit. You brag, 'I'm rich, I've got it made, I need nothing from anyone,' oblivious that in fact you're a pitiful, blind beggar, threadbare and homeless" (Rev. 3:15-17, *THE MESSAGE*).

Hear and heed.

Priorities: Churches Overlook Needs

In times of tight budgets and declining attendance, many churches overlook the needs of children and their parents. The reasoning goes like this: Things are tight and we have no young families; let's give up that ministry for now. Usually it never is reinstated. Soon the church has few children or young families and wonders why.

Apathy: Churches Are Too Tired to Care

When pastors get together, they often discuss the apathy of the laity toward children's ministries. The problem may grow out of hectic schedules, poor recruitment strategies or lack of information concerning the needs of a child or children. Every church can predict its slow but sure extinction by the degree of apathy and indifference shown to children and their needs.

Personnel: Who Will Serve the Children?

Recruiting qualified people to serve in any assignment seems harder now than ever before during a time when the need for volunteers to serve children is growing day by day.

Awareness: Canvass the Community

Sometimes a church does not provide ministry for its children because no one takes the time to discover the needs in the community around the church. Any problem any kid has anywhere in America is either already present, or it shortly will be, in every community.

Purity: Sin Bars Ministry Doors

For two centuries, the Christian Church has dealt with the problem of denouncing sin while being willing to care for the sinner along with the consequences that sin brings.

Generational Tension: Diversity Is Essential

Some churches have so directed their ministry toward a certain age group that they only know how to minister to that age group. As kids grow, the prospects of retaining an extended family at church shrink.

Survival: Paying Bills Confused with Ministry

Many churches are committed to survival rather than to ministry. Their primary efforts and resources are directed toward keeping the doors open. Such a mentality does not leave much room or interest for serving children.

THERE IS MORE TO MIND THAN BUSINESS

The church must lead in a new reformation to protect children—even when critics cry, "We'll take care of the kids; let the church mind her business." Unfortunately, that is exactly what the church is doing: minding its business. Yet, children are the church's business, its main business. Jesus' warning is clear as crystal: "Take heed that you do not despise one of these little ones" (Matt. 18:10, *NKJV*).

The church must keep asking itself why children should be its main business. The reasons are strongly related to every church's mission:

- The directives of Scripture
- The assignment from Jesus
- The needs of hurting children
- The absence of parenting skills
- The moral vacuum of society
- The future of civilization

Now, more than ever, children and their families need genuine support and creative resources from communities, businesses and government. But most of all, they need what only the church can provide. Every church that responds redemptively to the cries of children can be part of a revolutionary spiritual force that will help provide children and their parents with a satisfying lives that flow from continual contact with Christ. The Church must add a significant spiritual component, such as a national call of renewal to nurture kids, or the momentum of our present destructiveness will not be slowed.

With a large secular generation bent on committing moral suicide, it's time for the Church to be the Church. With two of the largest denominations in moral disgrace, one with pedophiles among its clergy and the other with a homosexual bishop, it's time for the Church to be the Church.

The Main Thing Must Remain the Main Thing

After every school massacre or disaster, the media provide clergy and churches high visibility, a golden opportunity to speak for God. These opportunities are an admission by our culture that the Christian faith should be considered during troubling circumstances.

Sadly, the replies churches give at times like these are often puny and bloodless. When given a secular audience and a TV camera, many members of the clergy give inane responses. In such settings, some religious leaders try to sound like secular psychologists, failing to explore the supernatural qualities of faith and life transformation. Others make public statements that sound like religious goofy dust—words and sentences calculated neither to offend nor to transform. While being careful not to offend, these speakers water down the awesome remedies of love and righteousness.

The Mission Must Be Discovered and Understood

Today, the Church's reason for existence may be a bit hard to identify. The massive changes in communities, churches and culture sometimes fog the issues. Thousands of Americans have little or no Christian memory, so they have no roots on which to evaluate a church's primary purpose. Pastors, laypeople and many students preparing for Christian ministry, who should be frontline soldiers in the revolution to save our children, are waiting to find out what God wants to accomplish. Some of these people have been waiting for a large part of their lifetime.

Barbara Brown Taylor, professor at Piedmont College in Demorest, Georgia, stated the problem in these words: "The church used to supply people with purpose, but I am afraid that we are going through a little slump right now. Some of our old purposes have run out of steam."[8]

Taylor continues to describe what we know is true: "If you walk into the average Christian church to explore your purpose, chances are that you will come out with an invitation to join the choir or volunteer at the soup kitchen on Tuesdays."[9]

The Church Must Refocus Now

The Church must get its act together, to refocus everything it does on Jesus. More emphasis on faith, hope and righteousness is needed. In these troubled times, all who claim the Christian name must plead on bended knee with the Father for repentance, renewal and restoration to a place of holy influence with transforming cultural results.

The Church cannot significantly impact the masses by merely doing more of what it has been doing. A Sunday School class that takes children on an information trip about biblical facts, as good as it may be, will never kindle the needed reformation. An entertainment-focused youth group will never equip young people for this spiritual battle. Neither will a denomination or association of churches energize a moral reformation by making more pronouncements about public policy.

The salt-in-the-wound, present-day prophet Tony Campolo wrote: "The church has the vision that is needed for the rebirth of America. . . . That vision has been fleshed out in the life of Christians portrayed in the book of Acts. . . . All that has to happen is for the church to be The Church and America will have what it needs to live again."[10]

A few paragraphs later, Campolo challenged the contemporary Church—that means us: "At its best the church is the only organization that exists solely for the good of its nonmembers. . . . The church must live up to its calling. A dying nation and a people who have lost their collective soul are depending on it."[11]

Every Church Must Accurately Assess Its Needs

We need something more than loud lament accompanied by vigorous hand-wringing. Our children, our culture and, ultimately, our civilization depend on our finding solutions to moral, spiritual and behavioral problems. In the assessment process, we must recognize that our churches have failed to help kids because they have failed to help the children's parents.

The family has been under sustained pressure for years. These moral gaps have produced a frightening, entangling—even choking—soul-destroying force into our society. Just as weeds, varmints, decay and dry rot take over abandoned buildings, wickedness, decay and avoidance overtake our families and churches. It is time for us to reclaim what has been lost. It is time for us to shout, "This is enough!" Make it stick. Then change it.

Don't Sweat the Small Stuff

In Littleton, Colorado, after the Columbine shootings, some members of the clergy criticized people who planned the memorial service, claiming it was too evangelical and too white. As a result, many shared *Denver Post* columnist Kathleen Parker's outrage as she scorched the moral landscape:

> On this day, such personal posturing trivializes the
> monumental loss of these families. . . . Listen up. You
> could expect better behavior from 10 toddlers with one
> cookie. . . . More important, how dare anyone exercise
> the arrogantly poor taste to criticize a memorial service
> only days after these kids were murdered and only hours
> after some were buried? What sort of spiritual leaders
> are these?[12]

Parker's question deserves a serious answer and requires a
profound change in attitude and action.

God Wants Faith-Filled Believers

Let's rethink what God wants from a church. Although many
people outside the Church have little interest in the institutional church, Jesus will attract them. A church's message about the
living Christ must be crafted so that it accurately describes a
quality life brimming with adventuresome fulfillment. Even
though believers know the Church is incredibly relevant to contemporary life, millions will remain disinterested unless their
nearby church speaks in ways they understand.

This requires Christlike qualities, which must be demonstrated so that a church is not guilty of doing what novelist John
Updike accused it of doing: "They promote thirst without
quenching it."[13] Every church must offer life-giving water to
thirsty souls. And that starts with serving children.

In the aftermath of the World Trade Center attacks and the
sniper shootings in Washington, D.C., thousands flocked to
houses of worship to pray and to revisit questions of faith and
purpose. They came seeking spiritual bread, divine comfort and
strength for coping. They flocked to sanctuaries—places of

refuge—to search for answers and to find faith. It is times like these when arguments about secularization of the masses, cynicism about the Church's influence, doubt about the reliability of Scripture and confusion about doctrine do not seem very important.

But that is not the whole story. In times of disaster, many congregations demonstrated what a church should be. Anyone who watched TV coverage following the tragedies at Columbine, Oklahoma City, New York and Washington, D.C., witnessed incredible dependence on God. Although not all people would agree with every jot of faith expressed on TV, it was hard not to rejoice with survivors of those tragedies who found strength in their personal relationship with Jesus and shared that discovery with the world. Like a high tide that lifts all ships in the harbor, the outpouring of faith helped the country begin the healing process.

More Than Ordinary Pastors and Churches Are Needed

Because the need is so great—children and their broken families are near the front door of every church—every ordinary pastor and every ordinary lay leader in every ordinary church must take his or her part in the mission to save our kids.

"They must stir us . . . ," Tony Campolo declared. "They must lead us . . . if they fail, we fail. . . . Those who head up the ministry of God's people in the world have an incredible responsibility to preach and teach the things that make for revival."[14]

It is time to pray, "Lord, what is my part in changing the world for all the children I know and for those near me that I don't know?" Or perhaps it is time to sing our prayer, especially the last phrase of this stanza of the hymn, "Spirit of the Living God":

I ask no dream, no prophet's ecstasies
No sudden rending of the veil of clay

No angel visitant, no opening skies
But take the dimness of my soul away.[15]

The Church Is Called to Encourage Relationships

The challenge to churches everywhere is not to fill the calendar
or to create more work for its people, but to place a new emphasis on developing healthy, Christ-centered relationships with
some of the most significant people in the population—children.
The idea is to direct the Church away from institutional preservation and toward meeting authentic human needs. Play down
the idea of another program. Emphasize the need for relational
efforts to revolutionize the next generation.

The good news: Serving children is something the Church
already knows how to do and the needed facilities are already in
place. When they were kids, many adults in every church were
loved to Christ by someone. Many of these people know how to
replicate what they experienced as a ministry to the new generation. This is a big-brother, big-sister type of relationship that can
grow spiritually strong people for the next generation.

THE CHURCH CAN REVOLUTIONIZE KIDS' LIVES

Pastor Rick Ezell, senior pastor at the Naperville, Illinois, Baptist
Church, told a story about the Green Bay Packers, who had been
hapless for 12 years before Vince Lombardi's arrival:

> The legendary coach turned his team into the dominant
> NFL team of the 1960s. Why such a phenomenal turn-
> around? Frank Gifford says it was not Lombardi's knowl-
> edge, since several coaches knew as much about strategy
> and tactics. Rather, it was his ability to motivate the play-

ers. "He could get that extra 10 percent out of an individual," Gifford says. "Multiply 10 percent times 40 men on the team times 14 games a season—and you're going to win."[16]

Now, do the math to determine the Church's potential. For example, multiply 340,000 churches by 20 people in each church by 52 Sundays. The result is a win-win situation. The key to such success, however, rests with church leaders who not only understand the opportunities that exist but also can motivate members of the congregation to reach out with deeds of kindness to kids in the name of Jesus.

We pray for children
who are cherished by their parents,
who grumble when pushed to try new foods,
who put off homework until bedtime;

and we pray for children
who relive 9/11 every time a plane flies overhead,
who pick the neighbor's tulips to give Mom a bouquet,
who live with aging grandparents because Mom has deserted
them and Dad is in jail.

CHAPTER 5

HOW TO BECOME A HERO OF HOPE

Wanted: Advocates for Children

Everyone loves a hero: a baseball pitcher who wins the Cy Young Award, a quarterback who throws a touchdown that wins the Super Bowl, a rock star who has a top 10 hit, a Hollywood celebrity who stars in a blockbuster movie, a firefighter who rescues someone from a burning building.

But children? What about all of God's children, including the hyperactive kids who disrupt services at church, refuse to sit still during Sunday School, run wild in the church hallways, snatch extra pieces of cake during the hospitality hour?

"Sure," you say, "they're okay in their place, but please keep them in their place."

Which calls to mind a story about the education department chairman of a great university who decided to pour a cement driveway at his house. In the process, he suffered blistered hands and back spasms. As you might suspect, kids in the neighborhood watched, waited and, when no one was looking, carved their names in the cement before it dried. The administrator was furious and grumbled loud and long to his wife.

"But I thought you loved children," she said.

"I love kids. I really do," he replied. "I love them in the abstract but not in the concrete."

Okay, the story may be old, but the message is clear: Our challenge is to really love kids—specifically and concretely. We can experience this love, for example, as we work with children in Sunday School. As one teacher commented: "Sometimes when I go all out for children, it is as if we were in heaven together, or at least in one of its suburbs."

Children wait in our churches, in our homes and in our communities for heroes to improve their lives.

Unfortunately, children still wait in our churches, in our homes and in our communities for heroes to improve their lives. They wait for an advocate to speak for them because they cannot represent themselves. They wait for someone like us to show them Jesus, the children's friend. They need people like us to be their heroes of hope.

Author Vance Packard warns: "The whole tilt of our society, our institutions and, yes, our family functioning is toward blighting our youngsters and burdening them with pain, anxiety and discouraging problems."[1]

We must take action, but how?

To sharpen our focus, we should think of a child we know, placing the name and face in our minds. Now, try to see the world and our church through the eyes of that particular kid.

We might choose a child from today's newspaper whose distress was reported on the front page. Perhaps it is the girl who barely missed being killed in a drive-by shooting. Or a boy who set fire to an apartment because he was playing with a lighter while his parents were at work. Or a boy who does not attend school because his parents are undocumented aliens. Or a kid whose mother was called to military service in one of the world's political hot spots.

Now we need to get fired up like columnist Rosemary Harris:

> I see a crusade in this place (our city, Colorado Springs), an onward-soldiers kind of crusade aimed at saving our young people. Sometimes crusades make me suspicious. But I don't see anything fake, patently political or self-serving about this one. There's too much at stake. . . . Our city could be a model for what a galvanized community can do for its future. Its children.[2]

Let's make the issues clear and "in your face," as the teens say. If we were children today, what would we need from the nearest Christian? We would need someone to represent our interests at school, at church and in the community. Kids don't have anyone from their age group elected to a public office or a place of leadership in their church. That is why they need us. Let's become a self-appointed ombudspersons for children in our communities, our churches and our cultures. The dictionary says an ombudsman investigates complaints, reports findings and mediates fair settlements.[3] What kids need are ombudspersons, heroes of hope, and we can be these heroes.

BEING AN AUTHENTIC CHRISTIAN

Kids need to be taught faith and wholeness. They need to be taught that breaking the commandments always produces harmful consequences. They need to have the harsh edges of faith criticism blunted and the unsatisfying results of secularism highlighted through what they see in people of faith and what they are taught at church and at home.

It is difficult for a child to doubt Christianity when they see

It is difficult for a child to doubt Christianity when they see it lived out in us.

it lived out in us. In an address to the Helping Children Follow Jesus Conference at Wheaton Graduate School, Dr. Virginia Patterson, president of the Southern Baptist Pioneers Clubs, said: "The single most important factor for contributing to resiliency in children was a consistent, long-term relationship with a significant adult or adults."[4]

Children and teenagers never forget people who live out dynamic faith. As adults who lead in our churches, Christian neighbors and adult family members, we have the opportunity to put an indelible imprint on the souls of children.

PROMOTING A USER-FRIENDLY ENVIRONMENT

The ideal childhood development program would be for the nation, schools, churches, communities, neighborhoods and every home to give children high priority. Too often kids feel unwanted at home, unwelcome at church and hassled at school. These are the children who most often join gangs, attach themselves to older sweethearts or become lifelong loners.

By high priority, we do not mean more tinkering with social policy. Rather, we mean the simple but significant priority of having individuals reach out to children. We mean adults becoming mentors to kids. We mean intentionally including children who have no family in our family's activities. We mean doing things illustrated by statements such as the one a single father made to several women in the church he attended: "I am a widower trying to be father and mother to my children. Thanks for teaching my daughters how to stand straight, walk like a lady and for including them in activities with your girls."

By high priority, we mean an older couple's becoming friends with some other person's child. In my (Neil's) growing-up years, lva and Charles Davidson were a childless couple who had married late in life. About once each month, they took me home for Sunday dinner. They talked about what interested me, about how to live, how to think and how to believe. They offered me a loan for my first semester in college. It is not hard to understand why they were among some of the most important people in my faith formation.

Mary lives out this principle in our city. Her kids are grown, and she and her husband are in their retirement years. Our newspaper reported that Mary feels a strong tie to the neighborhood school that gave her children a superior education. So, "most days you can find her at school, reading to children, helping them select library books, being a caring grand friend." The article continued, "It puzzles Mary that more retirees with time on their hands and public school success in their children's histories aren't doing the same thing."[5]

What has Mary discovered that she could teach individuals at our church? She has learned the lesson that Margaret Mead, famous anthropologist and authority on primitive cultures, taught: "Of course we need children. Adults need children in their lives to listen to and care for, to keep their imagination fresh and their hearts young and to make the future a reality for which they are willing to work."[6]

In a nearby town, a crew was assembled for an old-fashioned barn raising for a church building. Can you imagine the impact it made on children who were allowed to do simple tasks, to eat with volunteers and to help with cleanup? In 20 years, the building committee leader for a new church may be one of those kids who collected wood scraps on that project.

Every child needs an adult to cherish him or her as a person of worth.

INTRODUCING A CHILD TO A LOVING SUNDAY SCHOOL TEACHER

Such a role model was a person whom everyone called Mary Q.

Mary Quackenbush made a serious faith commitment to Christ when she was 75 years old. She became an enthusiastic, dedicated, faithful teacher of 10-year-old girls.

Surely, if anyone had valid reasons for not teaching children, Mary had them—age, health, etc. Yet she continued to teach week after week. And then there was the matter of experience. On many occasions Mary, who was a new Christian, could not answer the kinds of questions that young girls can raise. But there she was, studying her lesson faithfully, consulting with her pastor when necessary and trusting God for the wisdom to deal wisely with those questions.

How did Mary approach her task of teaching the young girls? Was she there only because her church was short of workers? Was she there only because she felt a sense of guilt or duty? No, she was there because she loved children and wanted to make a difference in their lives. I (Neil) know because I was Mary's pastor, and I caught her enthusiasm for ministry as I spoke with her.

The number one requirement for a Sunday School teacher is love for kids, and that spiritual instinct comes from close association with our loving Lord.

STRENGTHENING AND SUPPORTING THE CHILD'S FAMILY

For children, an extended family or something like it is absolutely necessary. But the extended family doesn't work very well these days because so many people live miles from grandparents, uncles, aunts and cousins. Add to this loss the large number of broken biological families, and we have big problems. The breakdown of the American family, especially during the last three decades, has been disastrous for children and has increased social problems that rob kids of security and emotional support at a time when both are needed the most.

In its finest hour, a church has a continual two-pronged ministry to families: (1) to strengthen existing families and (2) to become a substitute family for those who have no family. The following list includes several ways ministry can be effective:

- Move alongside to strengthen marriages
- Help parents who fail at parenting
- Love children from broken families
- Become a substitute family

SPEAKING UP FOR REFORM

Today, Christians are making their voices heard and their votes count in national and local elections. Many people who oppose this new force for righteousness have influenced elections for years but now are calling these new efforts a foul ball—as if making public officials aware of the citizens' concerns were not as old as America and a healthy expression of democracy. After all, the cornerstone of our national life is government by the people and for the people.

More individuals and more groups must represent children in halls of government and in halls of schools. Many special-interest groups have representatives and funding sources to make their wishes known to elected officials, but children must count on adults to speak for them. Although they are kids for such a short time, what happens in childhood shapes them forever. The Church must speak up, not to control the votes, but to be sure truth and values based on that truth are built into the fabric of America. Of course, Christian people will not agree on every detail of every issue, but they can produce a groundswell to ensure that righteousness serves as the controlling factor for all public policy.

A commitment to insist that the needs of children be considered in all public forums has to be considered the duty of every believer. Physician Lee Salk once passionately wrote:

> The cost to society of children whose lives have been damaged by poor nutrition, poor educational opportunities, poverty and poor health management is devastating. Ignoring these problems in the face of all the knowledge we have about the factors that contribute to their causes is beyond belief when we think of the resource, power and supposed wisdom of our elected officials.[7]

Dr. Salk's statement is true. But his outrage must be broadened to include our failure to attend to spiritual commitments and moral issues. Pastors, Christian education administrators and teachers must say with the Early Church, "For we cannot but speak the things which we have seen and heard" (Acts 4:20, *NKJV*).

Focus on the Family has served children well as it has urged Christian people to become advocates for children at various levels of civic and national life.

Because the Church has a significant responsibility to kids, it should see to it that communities are kid friendly.

Advocacy basically means the Church actively asks every part of society to make it possible for children to feel safe and cherished. Advocacy efforts for children need not be grand or big. We may be surprised at how responsive government leaders will be to our concerns if we express them kindly, insistently and frequently. Every member of every church can do some-

Every member of every church can do something so that children are treated better.

thing so that children are treated better and more kindly.

Advocacy Has Many Faces

Advocacy may mean organizing a program for cable TV to make people aware of the needs of children. It may mean serving on committees of the PTA or school board. It may mean organizing a forum of community leaders to make our communities more aware of kids' needs. Or it may mean calling on a government official to ask how we can help.

Advocacy May Be Simple

Advocacy may be as easy as offering our church's facilities for the use of community groups, such as Alcoholics Anonymous

(A.A.), Mothers Against Drunk Drivers (MADD), or Boy Scouts of America. Or it may be providing support for information groups for parents of children with disabilities or disease.

Advocacy Starts with Awareness

Sometimes, advocacy is merely offering a program to inform people about what is happening in our communities that harms children. At other times, it is taking the part of a child who needs someone to speak for him or her in school or in the community. Or maybe it means calling attention to harmful bureaucratic practices of social service agencies that deal with foster care or adoptions.

STARTING WITH THE FAMILY OF GOD

I. B. Priestley's classic play *An Inspector Calls* has been playing for years in London's West End. The play opens with a middle-class father, Arthur Birling, telling his grown son Eric and his future son-in-law Gerald Croft that young men have a right to live in the fast lane, where all do whatever seems right to them. Then Police Inspector Goole enters and informs the three men that a young woman named Eva Smith has committed suicide.

Seeking to build a case, Goole tells the three men about Eva's several aliases, shows her picture to them and asks many probing questions. As the play continues, every character comes to believe he or she had a part in Eva's death. Arthur Birling has been her employer and had fired her for participating in a worker-organized strike. Sheila Birling, his daughter, had had a selfish fit because she thought Eva, then employed at a dress shop, had laughed at her, so she complained to the shop owner, who fired Eva. During the inspector's questioning, it turns out that Gerald had had an affair with Eva but later had broken it off. Mr. Birling, Sheila and Gerald feel responsible for the death—all for different reasons.

Then enters Sybil Birling, a society matron and mother of Sheila. She heads a social service organization that had denied help to Eva because she was pregnant and unmarried, though Sybil did not know that her son Eric was the unborn child's father.

For a large part of the play, it appears that Eva was strongly influenced to take her life by the job losses Mr. Birling and Sheila caused, by the rejection of Gerald, by Mrs. Birling's refusal of her request for help and by the hopelessness caused by Eric's actions. What a mess for one family!

As the London *Evening Standard* reported, "When Inspector Goole arrives to question the Birlings about a young woman's death, it is not long before he discovers the whole family shares responsibility for her."[8] All members of the family become victims as they victimize others.

This is true about today's kids, too. But it can be changed. Through the strengths of the family of God, we can provide resources, and revitalize and renew broken families. In the process we can provide children opportunities they might not experience otherwise.

If we are to save the children, we must become their heroes of hope.

PART 2

THE AMAZING POWER OF GOD'S FAMILY

We pray for children
who are taught by gifted teachers in good schools,
who can have any kind of sports equipment they want,
who try to sneak to the supper table without
washing their hands;

and we pray for children
who fear that they might not live to grow up,
who do not live with their family of origin because
of divorce or abuse,
who try not to cry when a friend gets beaten by
a gang member.

CHAPTER 6

FAMILY TRAITS OF KID-SENSITIVE CHURCHES

Boys and Girls Loved Here

A number of years ago my wife and I (Neil) traveled through a small mountain town en route to a ministry assignment in another state. As we drove down Main Street we saw a hand-lettered sign that read "Children loved here." It was posted in front of a tiny church where the aging pastor and his wife were standing on the front steps welcoming children. Lots of them.

My thoughts were drawn to those incredibly assuring words from Scripture: "What marvelous love the Father has extended to us! Just look at it—we're called children of God! That's who we really are" (1 John 3:1, *THE MESSAGE*).

I heard my friend T. Crichton Mitchell, now with the Lord, preach from that sentence, "That's who we really are." He said, "There ought to be a way of lining up a regiment of exclamation marks, like the flag bearers at the Olympics, to lead in for public display the unspeakable marvel of the love of God!"[1]

Children of God! That's who we really are. Today's kids need to be loved by a church that rejoices in this incredible reality. Such a church creates a magnetic attraction for hurting children and broken families as well as for healthy families and happy kids. Any church can qualify by cultivating the following eight family traits.

FAMILY TRAIT 1: MINISTRY TO FAMILIES IS TIED CLOSELY TO A CHURCH'S MISSION

Ministry to children and families is an incredibly pressing contemporary challenge facing a church. The number of people affected and the intensity of their pain calls for an all-out response. Although many congregations offer family ministries, something much deeper and more essential is needed. The ministry to children and families stands at the heart of a church's reason for existence. This focus and commitment also needs to show in the spirit of individuals and the congregation. Such a church ministers to families by the way people relate to one another in the various expressions of ministry, by the way people are cherished and by the way a church's loving atmosphere spills over into the atmosphere of the homes.

It is a community of faith that could be called the society of Jesus. He is the leader. He is in control, and people love it that way. And this society loves Him so much that its members are eager to tell others what they have seen and heard, like the Early Church in Acts 4:20.

In his book *The Family-Friendly Church,* family counselor and pastor Dr. Richard Dobbins identifies two methods of accomplishing this mission: "My hope for the family of God is firmly anchored in my conviction that the family of God must become a surrogate family for those whose families are broken and, at the same time, must remain a strong spiritual source for those whose families are intact."[2]

Those two dimensions of a church's mission—better families and becoming family to those who have no family—strengthen and support each other. To settle for one without the other would waste ministry opportunities that would reach a great percentage of the population.

The two components worked well for a little girl named Amy. She was in kindergarten when she started traveling to Sunday School in the blue church bus. One Sunday, her shy, soft-spoken Sunday School teacher introduced Amy to Jesus. Amy immediately began inviting her mother to church but received no promises that she would attend. Much to her surprise, her mother eventually visited her church. Amy's mother asked Christ to be her Savior on that first Sunday. Later, Amy's grandmother came to faith. And 17 years later her grandfather became a believer.

Now grown and serving as a Sunday School teacher, Amy said, "Four in my family came to Christ because of the faithful witness of my Sunday School teacher. All that time we prayed for my grandfather were years when we had a better family because of the church, even as we waited and prayed for his salvation."

Her church had become a surrogate family to Amy until she could develop her own spiritually strong, intact family that now serves children, just as she once was served.

What a blessing it is to experience the excitement generated by a ministry to families. What an affirming environment to help children formulate faith. What an opportunity for children to become acquainted with people who model God's grace and faithfulness. Preaching, teaching, evangelism and worship for children and adults are always more effective in warm family churches.

FAMILY TRAIT 2: A CHURCH EMBODIES FAMILY MINISTRY

Although every church may be similar to other groups in society, God intended for His people to be uniquely relational and redemptive. He intended for His Church to remain spiritually healthy by the soul-shaping exercises of loving acts and life-changing relationships among its members. God envisioned a church where people know one another by name, a place where children feel they belong and a place where members frequently meet to celebrate the accomplishments of their heavenly Father and their elder brother, Jesus (see Rom. 8:29; Hebrews 2:11).

Some church members argue that it is a mistake to call a church a family, even though Paul used the term. Of course, the most blatant false advertising in the world would be to call some churches a family. Unfortunately, some church leaders who use the term "family" have never experienced authentic family relationships themselves.

Despite these differences, every church must respond like a caring family to the cries of children everywhere. It must be a place where kids and parents are lovingly adopted and fully accepted into the family of God.

The following is a list of programs and ministries that have worked in various churches:

- Intergenerational whole-family strategies
- Support groups for specialized needs such as singles groups that give attention to the different needs of the 18-year-old single person and the 80-year-old widow
- Workshops on understanding one's sexuality
- Parenting-skills seminars
- Single-parenting workshops
- Building networks for family needs

- Support groups for nurture and service
- Boys and girls weekend clubs
- Life-purpose classes
- Annual family-life conference
- Marriage-preparation classes
- Home-improvement workshops
- Building-faith-at-home workshops

FAMILY TRAIT 3: A CHURCH IS NOT INTIMIDATED BY INSTABILITY AND DIVERSITY

Churches are often maligned for not doing more about the problems that kids face. At first glance, that evaluation may sound accurate. But on further look, the great hindrances that can cause inaction in a church may be confusion about what constitutes a family, so-called alternative lifestyles and the widely accepted notion that government can solve family problems.

Or the confusion may reflect a serious desire to keep a church pure from the world. That kind of church will find it easy or perhaps even desirable to ignore the spiritual and emotional needs of children who are not members of traditional two-parent families.

Children Are Victims

Of course, a church cannot approve of every family arrangement that the world embraces. At the same time, Christ calls the Church to recognize that children in the most shocking circumstances need the Church more than anyone else. When kids are damaged by their parents' destructive lifestyles, our churches must move beyond their comfort zone to help, like Jesus did in talking with the woman at the well (see John 4).

Families Are Often Fragmented

"The ideal family is getting hard to come by," according to a comment in a national survey. "But . . . what's left of the family—whether it's a father and son, mother and children, or whatever—you can still have a lot of working together and playing together."[3]

While suggesting ways churches can accept and help single parents and broken families, Dr. James Dobson said:

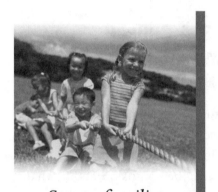

If I understand biblical imperatives correctly, it is the task of intact families and churches to extend a helping hand. The Lord has a special place in His heart for widows (including rejected husbands and wives) and fatherless children.[4]

Strong families build strong churches, and strong churches build strong families.

Congregations Need to Serve Needy Children

No congregation should feel guilty because it is unable to serve the needs of all children, but it should be deeply troubled if it is making no attempt to save some children. A starting place is to realize that every child needs a church like God wants His to be.

Surely, every church can do such things as minister to an infant with AIDS contracted at birth, reach out to a single teenaged mother and her baby, do something to help abused women and their children, and love troubled kids. Every church can also provide an event like a mother's day out for women who are overstressed from spending 24 hours a day with their preschool-aged children, make available a place for latchkey kids who would otherwise go home to empty houses every day or find a volunteer or two to work in a troubled school.

FAMILY TRAIT 4: FAMILY AND CHURCH NEED TO SUPPORT EACH OTHER

Strong families build strong churches, and strong churches build strong families. A church should make every effort to help families learn to live out their Christian life. Richard Olson and Joe H. Leonard, Jr., coauthors of *A New Day for Family Ministries*, suggest that many troubled families will be grateful when they find a church that does the following:

- Offers hope for what families can become
- Provides advocacy for families
- Confronts abusive behavior
- Offers training and information about marriage
- Helps families aspire to be all that they can be.[5]

That list needs to have the transformation of the gospel added as its highest priority.

FAMILY TRAIT 5: KID-SENSITIVE CHURCHES BUILD STRONG FAMILIES

Authentic New Testament churches do everything they can to build strong families.

Avoid Hyperfamilism
Two fears are frequently voiced today about the relationship between family and church. Some church leaders fear that

churches can become so family oriented that other Kingdom interests will be short-changed. Others fear that church schedules will be so filled that family members will have little time to spend together in the home.

A balance is needed but may be difficult to achieve. Author Rodney Clapp is credited with coining the term, "hyperfamilism," which describes a commitment to enriching the family at the expense of other interests and responsibilities.[6]

I (Neil) once served a wonderful family who bought a weekend mountain cabin at which to spend time as a family. But they used it so frequently that their children seldom attended church and lost interest in church. They put family first in an out-of-balance way, and while their goal of family time was accomplished, they failed in their primary goal of encouraging their kids to develop personal relationships with Christ.

View Marriage and Service as a Way to Find Fulfillment
Charles Sell, a Christian family-life specialist and Trinity Evanglical Divinity School professor, offers these observations about a reasonable but healthy connection between home and church:

> God has given us all things to enjoy, including marriage and family. Certainly we should not allow our enjoyment of marriage to interfere with our commitment to church . . . But neither should we permit enjoyment of church to the neglect of our family life, as when church members immerse themselves in church work at the expense of their spouses and children.[7]

The goal in all of this is to be sure home and church each add to the strength of the other. Pastor Paul Caminiti writes,

"Parents were commanded to teach and talk to their children 'when you *sit* in your house, when you *walk* by the way, when you *lie down,* and when you *rise* up' (Deut. 6:7, *NKJV*, emphasis added). I like to think of these as 'home-grown' verbs. They convince me God is unhappy with rampant absenteeism that prevails in too many of our families."[8]

FAMILY TRAIT 6: KID-SENSITIVE CHURCHES WORK HARD TO BE SURROGATE FAMILIES

Certainly, the home and the church need to work together to save children from unhealthy homes, Christian and non-Christian alike.

We see that God planned for the family and their church to work together to nurture children spiritually. Problems arise when one partner—either the home or the church—fails to carry out its responsibilities or attempts to usurp the role of the other partner.

Unfortunately, as Michael S. Lawson and Robert J. Choun, Jr., point out, many families fail to carry out their biblical mandate to provide spiritual nurture for children, which places even more responsibility on a church: "The modern collapse of the family puts the church squarely in the position of needing to strengthen both the family unit and the individuals within it."[9]

It is a tough task for our churches to shoulder the heaviest end of this crushing load. But for many children, this strengthening will not be carried out if a church doesn't provide it. This increasingly heavy task is a wonderful place for a church to demonstrate how the love of God works through relationships in His family.

FAMILY TRAIT 7: A CHURCH SHOULD MAINTAIN AN ACCEPTING ENVIRONMENT FOR KIDS

The pressing question here is, Are children welcome at our churches? The need for kid-sensitive environments makes us examine our attitudes as well as our facilities, equipment and personnel. A kid-sensitive church strives to create a loving climate where all kinds of families feel comfortable: traditional families, blended families, single-parent families, children without families, adoptive families, foster families, no-children couples, bicultural families and singles.

A Church Should Give Children Priority

Kid-sensitive churches give children priority and significance. This might include such things as children's singing in the services, ushering and reading Scripture in adult services. In these churches, the ministry to children is highly visible, and facilities are well marked. Nursery facilities are located near the entrance, and grandparent-like volunteers reach out to children in the hallways.

These churches view kids as the Church of today as well as the Church of tomorrow. They work hard to know children's names and to provide a safe haven for them, some of whom have lived in brokenness their entire lives.

Kid-sensitive churches give attention to special needs. For example, they are aware that children from blended families may not be able to attend church functions as often as those who live in unbroken families. In this case, Sunday School lessons may be taught as single lessons rather than continued from Sunday to Sunday.

A Church Should Make Children Feel Welcome

Providing an intentional network for newcomers often is important in ministry to children. That may mean finding a substitute grandparent contact. It may mean putting a newly divorced parent in touch with a parent who worked through a divorce with their local church's help. Or it may mean putting a couple with their first baby in touch with a couple who has a one-year-old child.

A few years ago, I (Neil) attended one of the historic churches in New York City for a worship service. The bulletin announced that a child would be dedicated to the Lord during that service. The pastor invited the child to invite his parents and grandparents to come forward and join him for the dedication. The pastor then asked the parents to bring their other children, and he requested that the Sunday School teacher who worked with toddlers in the church nursery to come forward. With these simple, thoughtful touches, the pastor tied the church and the family together. The unspoken words were, "Children are important here" and "We cherish families."

A Church Should Listen to Children and Learn from Them

The older and larger a church becomes, the more it tends to make the gospel complicated. One devotional writer of another generation spoke longingly of returning to the simplicity of the primitive New Testament Church.

One solution to the difficulty of not knowing how to share the gospel with kids is to listen and to learn from children—hear what moves them, what worries them and what brings them joy.

The simplicity, purity and childlikeness of the New Testament Church appear to be something God wants us to imitate. Here is the way our Lord explained it: "I'm telling you, once and for all, that unless you return to square one and start over like children, you're not even going to get a look at the kingdom, let alone get in. Whoever becomes simple and elemental again, like this child will rank high in God's kingdom" (Matt. 18:3-4, *THE MESSAGE*).

FAMILY TRAIT 8: THE CHURCH BECOMES THE CHILD'S EXTENDED FAMILY

Increasing numbers of children do not live near their extended families, but they still need uncles and aunts, cousins and grandparents to affirm, hug, encourage, teach, love, cheer and sometimes spoil them. They need an extended family in times of joy as well as in times of sadness.

Every church can become like an extended family in a child's life. In every ministry, structure and mode of operation, a church can implement ways to become a family to families.

We love the tender idea Jack and Judith Balswick expressed by closing their book *The Family: A Christian Perspective on the Contemporary Home* with this Scripture reference: "When Jesus therefore saw His mother, and the disciple whom He loved standing by, He said to His mother, 'Woman, behold your son!' Then He said to the disciple, 'Behold your mother!' And from that hour that disciple took her to his own home" (John 19:26-27, *NKJV*).

The Balswicks also suggest, "Our goal in relationships should be to so forgive, empower and intimately know one another so that Jesus would want to send His mother to be a part of our family."[10]

For the purposes of developing an adopted extended family

in our churches, let's rephrase the Balswicks' sentence: The goal for relationships in our churches should be to so forgive, love and intimately care for children that Jesus would want every child to be a part of the family of God that meets at your church.

Every church can become like an extended family in a child's life. In every ministry, structure and mode of operation, a church can implement ways to become a family to families. It can welcome children, teens, unmarried people, orphans, blended families, newlyweds and people from every generation.

LET'S TRY SHOWING LOVE TO BIG MART

Big Mart lived in a changing New Jersey neighborhood where Don Bakely was pastoring a congregation of aging middle-class people who were out of touch with the neighborhood—especially with teens and children, some of whom were gang members. So Bakely talked with these youths, even wrestled with them and finally convinced them to attend church occasionally.

The first day Big Mart entered the church, he had a heated argument with the church secretary and called her a foul name. Ella, who also was the reigning matriarch of the congregation, marched into Bakely's office and demanded, "What are you going to do with that gang member in my office?"

"That's a good question," Bakely responded. "But the more pressing issue is, What are you going to do about it?"

"I want you to throw him out now," she said.

"Ella," the pastor said, "I've been working for six weeks to get [Big] Mart in here. I just can't throw him out until you have at least heard his story."

"Tell me," she replied.

Here's what Bakely told her: "When Big Mart was a small boy, his father came home one night and beat his mother to death. He was so violent that he insisted the children watch him kill their mother. After the murder, the father cut her head off in front of the children. That's right—he made them watch. When Big Mart could stand it no more, he ran for the door and started down the steps of their apartment building. His father became so enraged that he threw the mother's head at Big Mart, which knocked him down the steps. He's the same guy who called you that bad name, Ella."

Ella left the room and then returned 20 minutes later. "I guess I'll just have to learn how to be called bad names," she said.

Later Bakely wrote: "That's the day the church began ministry to its neighborhood youth."[11]

Although we may never meet a Big Mart in our neighborhoods, we can find many children and teens like him who have never been loved. There are children who know nothing about God. In every setting, there are kids who will be secularized on the outside and empty on the inside if a church doesn't reach them and their families soon.

We need to look around in every direction in search of children who need a church to love them, a Sunday School to teach them, a family to cherish them and a Christ-centered group to accept them. Their future depends on it, the future of the nation depends on it and the future viability of our churches depend on it, too.

We pray for children
who sneak cookies and hate vegetables,
who sleep with the cat but never walk the dog,
who love school except when it's time to get up;

and we pray for children
who have toothaches but no money for dentistry care,
who stare through barred windows into a seedy,
rundown neighborhood,
who have lost a playmate to a drive-by shooting.

FAMILY OF GOD ACCORDING TO SCRIPTURE

Developing the Biblical Pattern in Our Churches

People who have been deeply wounded by family problems are present everywhere these days.

I (Neil) overheard a one-way telephone conversation in a Boca Raton, Florida, department store. A woman salesperson was obviously talking to her significant other.

"I don't care what you think or what the kids want," she said. "We are common law, and that means I can come and go when I want to. You and the kids just have to understand that. No more discussion." For days I thought a lot about her children and about her future.

Miles from Florida, I was enjoying my hobby of people watching on a busy street near the convention center in Indianapolis where I was attending a ministers' seminar. As I watched, I saw a slender teenaged girl, who maybe weighed 95 to 100 pounds and could easily have passed for 12 or 13. In fact, she was sucking her thumb as she propositioned a man old enough to be her father, maybe her grandfather. Since then, I have wondered how she had fallen so far at such a young age. And I wondered if she had ever known there is a better, much better, lifestyle.

In New Mexico, I met a woman in her late 60s who said, "I had my first child at 16, and I didn't know much about parenting. I made lots of mistakes, and now the kids hate my guts. I never hear from them, and when I call, they often refuse to take the call or don't call me back. Does God have anything to help my pain?"

In a less drastic situation, I met a young father in a small New England inn a few days after 9/11. The ruggedly handsome, well-dressed young man appeared troubled as we talked. He said he was a salesman who sold large insurance policies to colleges and universities. He had an appointment the next morning that could result in a substantial commission.

"But I don't want to be there," he said. "This isn't what's important anymore. I want to be home with my wife and baby in New York City."

Then he told me (Neil) about himself:

I left home when I was 18 to seek my fortune in New York City. I've been back to my parents' home very few times. My extended family didn't seem to matter much to me. Five years ago, I married the girl of my dreams. Year before last, we decided to start our family. The baby, Shelly—we call her Junior because she looks like me—just turned 18 months. All summer the three of us took the stroller and walked to parks and did together what a young family does. What fun.

Now all this fear. This uncertainty. Now, business isn't important. Now, home, family, relationships and even my extended family are a high priority with me. My career can wait. I want to be with my family. I've starting thinking about faith, church and values.

As we talked, it was clear that he had lofty dreams for his family, but he had little spiritual experience or strength from his childhood—or anywhere else—to fall back on when parenting turns tough, as it will. Family really mattered to him now. He had discovered a law of relationships, equally valid to the law of gravity in physics.

DEVELOPING A NEW SENSITIVITY TO SPIRITUAL ISSUES

Each of these incidents represents millions of people, including those who are confused about what really matters in their lives. This New Yorker especially longed for family and meaning. But he didn't know how to develop a

Nearly 80 percent of Americans say family has become a higher priority for them since 9/11.

family because he lacked experience, spiritual memory or awareness of Scripture.

His yearning fits the findings of New York-based American Demographics and Greenwich, Connecticut-based marketing research firm NFO WorldGroup that discovered nearly 80 percent of Americans say family has become a higher priority for them since 9/11.

What an opportunity for our churches. But are we ready to seize it?

Family specialist Paul Pearsall said, "Families are not

failing, but we are failing families."[1] He is right, and each church must accept its share of the blame. To meet the crisis of spiritually needy children, thousands of contemporary churches need to do more "familying." The term means strengthening family, welcoming new believers into the family of God, and happily making room for and accepting unattached people who do not have a natural family. It means helping everyone with parenting, grandparenting and extended family skills. The Church, at its best, becomes very much like a caring extended family that gives to and receives love from everyone it touches.

In such an effort, everyone is enriched: those who receive, those who give and those who observe. The Church has a God-given capacity for assimilating and nurturing, and that capacity needs to be valued, used and expanded.

GETTING A CLEAR FOCUS ON THE MEANING OF FAMILY

Family is God's idea. He created it. Scripture frequently uses family words to describe relationships. Although the family of God is delightful to experience, it is hard to define.

The family of God offers a relationship, a place to belong. It is a supportive connection with brothers and sisters committed to Christ. They encourage and enable healthy character strengths like trust, honesty, love, loyalty and forgiveness to grow in us. The family of God is also a place to be loved and a faith development cradle for the young in age and the babes in Christ. It is a spiritual home where love and acceptance greatly exceed Robert Frost's definition: "Home is the place where, when you have to go there, they have to take you in."[2]

CREATING A NEW TESTAMENT FAMILY

Although the family unit in contemporary society has been battered, beaten and left for dead like the man on the Jericho Road
(see Luke 10:30-37), Scripture offers a blueprint for healing and
renewal. The family-like characteristics so often highlighted in
the Bible motivate us to find ways to reenergize the family of
God, especially in its service to children.

Halford Luccock's comments concerning Acts 1:13 inspire a
new appreciation for the tender bonds within the family at
church. This verse of Acts in the *New International Version* may
seem routine, perhaps a bit boring, on first reading: "Peter, John,
James and Andrew; Philip and Thomas, Bartholomew and
Matthew; James son of Alphaeus and Simon the Zealot, and
Judas son of James." Although the verse admittedly sounds
somewhat uninspiring, Luccock draws a surprisingly memorable perspective on family from the passage:

> Listen to the roll call in the upper room at Jerusalem, as
> we catch echoes of it in the 13th verse of the first chap-
> ter of Acts. Then consider this thought: Take away four
> families from this first Christian church and what do
> you have left?
>
> Here was the Zebedee family with James and John
> on the official board. Here was another family with the
> brothers Peter and Andrew. Here was some of Jesus'
> own family. It is a perfect picture of what most church-
> es are. Here are the Joneses, the Browns, the Robinsons
> and the Smiths. Just a family church but as such it fol-
> lows the original pattern of the most tremendous force
> in history.
>
> Christianity found its most transforming influence
> in primary human institutions. The family church has a

great inheritance. It should lift itself up to a new sense of worth and importance. What did Jesus leave to the world? Much in every way. But high among His greatest legacies was this—He left a family church.[3]

Once again we see that strong, supportive connection between family and church that follows us throughout so much of Scripture. Luccock calls family "the original pattern of the most tremendous force in history." What a force it is, and how badly we need that force to be revived in society today. Every child needs to experience firsthand the loving force of a caring congregation.

APPLYING SCRIPTURAL PRINCIPLES AS THE FAMILY OF GOD

Holy Scripture places high value on families on nearly every page. It speaks of Jesus' relationships to His earthly kin, to His adopted family composed of His disciples and to His extended family of followers consisting of all who do God's will. The fatherhood of God is mentioned frequently in Scripture, along with the wonderful good news that we are His sons and daughters. Jesus extols childlikeness as a worthy pattern for serving Him and others.

The Bible teaches repeatedly that because children are of supreme importance to God, they must be important to us. That means we must love kids, cherish them, train them and develop them. They must be led to develop their full potential in Christ. God expects the Church to lead in this adventure of helping people find the best life known to the human family.

Let's explore scriptural principles that will help us maximize the strength the family of God can provide children.

Principle 1: God Created the Family

According to the biblical record, God created families. Instruction for families soon followed in the first chapter of Genesis:

> So God created man in his own image, in the image of God he created him; male and female he created them. God blessed them and said to them, "Be fruitful and increase in number; fill the earth and subdue it. Rule over the fish of the sea and the birds of the air and over every living creature that moves on the ground" (vv. 1:27-28, *NIV*).

Children are created by God in His image, with potential for becoming vital persons in His kingdom. Listen in holy awe to Psalm 139:14-15 (*THE MESSAGE*):

> I thank you, High God—you're breathtaking!
> Body and soul, I am marvelously made!
> I worship in adoration—what a creation!
> You know me inside and out,
> you know every bone in my body;
> You know exactly how I was made, bit by bit,
> how I was sculpted from nothing into something.

And as part of His incredibly creative effort, the master designer endowed each child with amazing resiliency and potential. Scientist Louis Pasteur said, "When I approach a child, he inspires in me two sentiments: tenderness for what he is, and respect for what he may become."[4]

Principle 2: God's Family Welcomes Everyone

Scripture supports the idea that everyone is welcome in the

Father's house. One incredibly clear promise announces: "In Christ's family there can be no division into Jew and non-Jew, slave and free, male and female. Among us you are all equal" (Gal. 3:28, *THE MESSAGE*).

All believers are part of God's forever family whom He welcomes to His Church. That includes Matthew the tax collector, Peter the fisherman, Thomas the doubter, the sisters of Lazarus, Joe the mechanic, Helen the school teacher, James the meat cutter and Mary the bank manager.

Jesus is quick to explain that childlikeness is required for anyone who wants to be part of His holy family.

Yet Jesus is quick to explain that childlikeness is required for anyone who wants to be part of His holy family. He is saying: "I'm telling you, once and for all, that unless you return to square one and start over like children, you're not even going to get a look at the kingdom, let alone get in" (Matt. 18:3, *THE MESSAGE*).

Principle 3: God's Family Reaches Across Generations
Love is to faith what blood is to life. Love is the main character trait of the heavenly Father's family. Think of the amazing possibilities. God provides love for His family. He requires love from His family. He empowers His family to love one another.

Listen to Scripture to hear what our Lord says about the power of love:

A new command I give you: Love one another. As I have loved you, so you must love one another. By this all men will know that you are my disciples, if you love one another (John 13:34-35, *NIV*).

Later, He said:

I've loved you the way my Father has loved me. Make yourselves at home in my love. If you keep my commands, you'll remain intimately at home in my love. That's what I've done—kept my Father's commands and made myself at home in his love (John 15:9-10, *THE MESSAGE*).

The apostle Paul wanted everyone to appreciate, participate in and experience the advantage of being a part of the family of God: "Let us not grow weary while doing good, for in due season we shall reap if we do not lose heart. Therefore, as we have opportunity, let us do good to all, especially to those *who are of the household of faith*" (Gal. 6:9-10, *NKJV*, emphasis added).

At the heart of the Christian gospel is an inclusive community of persons who care for one another and for needy persons around them, especially children. It is the kind of caring that shows through Amy Carmichael's prayer:

> *Father, hear us, we are praying.*
> *Hear the words our hearts are saying.*
> *We are praying for our children.*
> *Keep them from the powers of evil,*
> *From the secret, hidden peril.*[5]

This inclusive community of caring is a fulfilling way to live and a blessed bonded relationship to cultivate. And it's a grand environment in which to rear children.

These relationships transcend generations. What wonderful assurance we have to know God keeps working across years and across generations. The Father of this forever family is the One who "keeps covenant and *mercy for a thousand generations* with those who love Him and keep His commandments" (Deut. 7:9, *NKJV*, emphasis added). Think about how long a thousand generations must be. God's faithfulness works longer than we can imagine in the lives of those people who have no idea God is answering the prayers of earlier generations.

Notice how Scripture joins "covenant" and "mercy" in this passage. Covenants are legal documents that communicate legal obligations that are to be legally implemented and followed. When Scripture places love and covenant together, we can be absolutely sure that God's love will be extended to us and to a thousand generations of people yet unborn.

Principle 4: The Family Offers New Beginnings

In Jesus Christ, God came into the world in human form to make it possible for us to be part of the Father's family.

Paul explains clearly in his Galatian letter:

> But when the fullness of the time had come, God sent forth His Son, born of a woman, born under the law, to redeem those who were under the law, that we might receive the adoption as sons. And because you are sons, God has sent forth the Spirit of His Son into your hearts, crying out, "Abba, Father!" Therefore you are no longer a slave but a son, and if a son, then an heir of God through Christ (Gal. 4:4-7, *NKJV*).

Scripture goes on to say:

This resurrection life you received from God is not a timid, grave-tending life. It's adventurously expectant, greeting God with a childlike, "What's next, Papa?" God's Spirit touches our spirits and confirms who we really are. We know who he is, and we know who we are: Father and children (Rom. 8:15-16, *THE MESSAGE*).

These words carry mind-boggling truth. We are no longer slaves because we have been adopted as sons and daughters. We have full family rights and privileges. Because we live in a holy, empowering relationship, God has made us heirs to His family resources and to the riches of heaven. Think of the implications for now and forevermore. Think of how many fatherless kids will delight to hear that good news.

Principle 5: The Family Extends Beyond Natural Bloodlines

"Long, long ago he decided to adopt us into his family through Jesus Christ. (What pleasure he took in planning this!)" (Eph. 1:5, *THE MESSAGE*).

Scripture reminds us that once, while Jesus was speaking to the multitudes, His mother and brothers showed up, wanting to speak to him:

Someone told Jesus, "Your mother and brothers are standing out here, wanting to speak with you." Jesus didn't respond directly, but said, "Who do you think my mother and my brothers are?" He then stretched out his hand toward his disciples. "Look closely. There are my mother and brothers. Obedience is thicker than blood. The person who obeys my heavenly Father's will is my brother and sister and mother" (Matt. 12:46-50, *THE MESSAGE*).

Scripture provides incredible words of grace to all who do the will of God. We can count on the promise that we are members of the family of Jesus if we do the will of the Father.

Principle 6: The Family Prospers
When Faith Is Taught and Caught

Living as a Christian is always harder when one is isolated from the family of faith's tender love and happy associations. That is one reason John Wesley taught that religion is never solitary. Through relationships, Christian faith is to be lived and learned and expressed in love.

A biblical teaching that represents this idea can be found in the instructions recorded in Deuteronomy 6:5-9 (*NKJV*):

> You shall love the LORD your God with all your heart, with all your soul, and with all your strength. And these words which I command you today shall be in your heart. You shall teach them diligently to your children, and shall talk of them when you sit in your house, when you walk by the way, when you lie down, and when you rise up. You shall bind them as a sign on your hand, and they shall be as frontlets between your eyes. You shall write them on the doorposts of your house and on your gates.

This Scripture sounds as if we are to constantly cultivate an awareness of the goodness of God and His bountiful provision for the human family and for the family of God. It also appears to challenge us to live in ways that attract children to God and to show them how faith works in the family.

An idea often overlooked in this passage is that those people who teach the truth to kids not only help the children but also help themselves by telling and retelling the good news. A 90-

year-old woman told us her worship experiences changed forever 60 years ago after she taught a lesson to third graders about how the ancient scribes were so awed by God that they always stopped to wash their pens before writing God's name in their manuscripts.

What you teach children often influences you profoundly.

Principle 7: The Family Thrives When It Gives Itself to Others

The Early Church learned to give richly by responding to every need it encountered. That lesson must be relearned in every generation: Giving makes the Church and those who are part of the Church richer, never poorer.

The contemporary family of God can't be satisfied to simply discuss the incredible problems kids face in our society. It is time to act. No more shaking our heads in surprise at what sin does to our children. It is time to move beyond dialogue to decisions.

It is time for action. Doing means caring. Caring means giving. Giving means making a difference. Action that produces life-changing achievement is needed now. This requires opening our hearts, our resources and our hands to children.

Doing means caring. Caring means giving. Giving means making a difference.

Throughout Christian history, the family of God has had few rivals in nurturing children. Wherever the Church has gone, it has ministered to the bodies, minds and souls of children, even as it has pointed them to Christ.

What has been done for kids across hundreds of years in mission settings must be replicated today in Western society, especially in urban settings. This is among our most urgent tasks.

Principle 8: The Family Develops People

How could anything be more affirming than the words of the apostle Paul:

> This kingdom of faith is now your home country. You're no longer strangers or outsiders. You belong here, with as much right to the name Christian as anyone. God is building a home. He's using us all—irrespective of how we got here—in what he is building (Eph. 2:19, THE MESSAGE).

Part of our job in the children's developmental process is to help them learn how to live. As Edmund Burke explained: "Society cannot exist unless a controlling power upon will and appetite be placed somewhere, and the less of it there is within the more there must be without."[6]

All kids need a church to accept and to love them even when they are not lovable. Such acceptance may require hard work, but the payoff can be unbelievably incredible.

Hear God's good news about human potential development—our own and that of others:

> But we all, with unveiled face, beholding as in a mirror the glory of the Lord, are being transformed into the same image from glory to glory, just as by the Spirit of the Lord. Therefore, since we have this ministry, as we have received mercy, we do not lose heart (2 Cor. 3:18—4:1, NKJV).

The payoff and accountability from serving children are stated almost poetically in Richard Lischer's book *The Preaching King,* which tells of Martin Luther King, Jr.'s childhood: "At Ebenezer Baptist Church, young King learned that when the preacher assumes his proper place in the hierarchy above the people and beneath the cross—and says what God wants him to say—the entire organism hums with power."[7]

CULTIVATING CHARACTERISTICS OF GOD'S FAMILY IN CHILDREN

Consider what the family of God means for contemporary people. Think about what it meant for ancient people. Imagine our fascination when we read a commentary about the family of God including Galatians 6:9-20 and Ephesians 3:14-15, two Scriptures from Paul. In 10 or 12 pages of Scripture, we put together this random list of traits of God's family, traits which the Church cultivates:

- Instruction and example
- Relationship with the Father
- Connection with spiritual siblings
- Discipline for holy living
- Promise of protection and safety
- Support when pain and grief come
- A family name, Christian
- Affirming affection

What a list of satisfying realities and relationships. Let us rejoice in these wonderful ties to the family of God and share them with the children we know. We must think of the potential available to millions of children who live their entire lives in despair and brokenness.

MAKING EVERY CHURCH A HOME FOR OUR SPIRITUAL DEVELOPMENT

One pastor welcomed new members into the fellowship of his church with the words, "Welcome to the forever family." What a perfect description of an authentic church in any age and especially in this time when mobility, divorce, alcoholism, infidelity and self-sovereignty have caused the spiritually damaging disintegration of the human family.

Scripture overflows with rich vocabulary about home and family as they relate to the Church. Brothers and sisters, fathers and mothers, reunions and a place called home are all part of its teaching.

As we researched biblical references for writing this book and let our minds soak in scriptural directives God has for the Church, we were amazed at the family warmth promised in passages such as these:

Home

"Live in me. *Make your home* in me just as I do in you" (John 15:4, *THE MESSAGE*, emphasis added).

Father

"I'm not writing all this as a neighborhood scold just to make you feel rotten. I'm writing as a father to you, *my children.* I love you and want you to grow up well, not spoiled" (1 Cor. 4:14, *THE MESSAGE*, emphasis added).

Adoption

"You can tell for sure that you are now *fully adopted as his own children* because God sent the Spirit of his Son into our lives crying out, 'Papa! Father!' " (Gal. 4:6, *THE MESSAGE*, emphasis added).

Children

"How great is the love the Father has lavished on us, that we should be called *children of God! And that is what we are!* The reason the world does not know us is that it did not know him" (1 John 3:1, *NIV*, emphasis added).

Family

"God's Spirit touches our spirits and confirms who we really are. We know who he is, and we know who we are: Father and children" (Rom. 8:16, *THE MESSAGE*).

Inheritance

"Doesn't that privilege of intimate conversation with God make it plain that you are not a slave, but a child? And if you are a child, you're also an heir *with complete access to the inheritance*" (Gal. 4:7, *THE MESSAGE*, emphasis added).

Reunion

"The Master himself will give the command. Archangel thunder! God's trumpet blast! He'll come down from heaven and the dead in Christ will rise—they'll go first. Then the rest of us who are still alive at the time will be caught up with them into the clouds to meet the Master. Oh, we'll be walking on air! And then there will *be one huge family reunion with the Master.* So reassure one another with these words" (1 Thess. 4:16-18, *THE MESSAGE*, emphasis added).

"Make your home in me just as I do in you" (John 15:4, *THE MESSAGE*). What a rich, lasting possibility that sentence portrays. Home suggests a friendly place to meet God and a special relationship that returns us to the simple, glorious roots of our faith.

And there is more.

In the future, we will be home during a huge family reunion with the master. The full meaning of this remembrance and anticipation is hard to imagine, but it inspires us to march on and to bring every child with us.

We pray for children
who ride in Mom's SUV with a "Kid's Taxi" bumper sticker,
who pretend to do homework while playing computer games,
who live in the big house on the hill and wear trendy sneakers;

and we pray for children
who have everything but no one to love them,
who are dying because medical help came too late,
who have never heard Bible stories.

CHAPTER 8

EMPOWERING THE PARTNERSHIP BETWEEN CHURCH AND HOME

Curse the Darkness or Light a Candle

Once a member of a church that I served as pastor shared with me a newspaper clipping from a California newspaper. It was reported as fact, and a convincing picture was published next to the article. The story reminds me of the message of this chapter.

"Thieves Steal Home!" read the headline. A house-moving company had put a house up on immense timbers on a large trailer and moved it to a new location during the night to avoid traffic snarls.

The movers encountered one major difficulty when they arrived—the foundation wasn't ready. So the house-moving crew decided to "store" the building on its trailer next to the huge hole that had been dug for the foundation. The next night, long before the foundation was ready, someone hitched the trailer to a diesel truck and stole the house.

A THREE-WAY PARTNERSHIP

This story sounds similar to the weakening partnership among the church, the home and the resources of God. While a church tries to figure out where the foundations for home are going to be, the home gets stolen. And when the home has been stolen, kids suffer the consequences.

Family specialist Charles Sell provides another, perhaps clearer, metaphor of this partnership in his call for an all-out effort to provide the mutually needed connection. Without it, Sell warns, "the Christian church and the Christian home are as closely bonded as Siamese twins. If they are cut apart, a major artery may be severed that causes one or both to hemorrhage or die."[1]

God intended for the family and their church to gain strength from one another. As we have seen in the Bible, God formed the biological family. He later established the family of God—the Church—on the Day of Pentecost. From that day until now, He has intended for church and family to fortify, augment and resource each other. The task of reinventing such a partnership to fit these times requires more savvy and strength than we have as individuals or as a group. We must have outside help. Help beyond ourselves. God's help.

Our situation reminds me of the story of a member of the Chicago Bulls basketball team, who was asked by the press, "What was your most memorable experience in playing on the same team as Michael Jordan?" He responded, "Oh, it was the night that Michael Jordan and I scored 70 points!"[2] What he didn't say was that Michael Jordan scored 69 points and he scored only 1.

That's the way our partnership with God works—we make one basket and He does the rest—all the rest. And He does it through us, if we let him.

A holy connection between God and human resources in this partnership is necessary in our churches and at home. T. S. Eliot puts it like this: "Where there is no temple, there shall be no homes."[3]

Too much of the work of a church in our time is mere human effort without the enablement of God. The sad shape of the family, their church and children in our time will never become much better until a church plugs in to the supernatural, transforming resources of God. Neither church nor home can survive for long without an inflow of new blood, new ideas and new commitments. We need to plug in to this holy connection between us and God for the sake of our kids.

Without a church, the family is impoverished, and without families, a church is beside the point—even irrelevant to life.

An Integral Partnership

As we begin to allow God to integrate this partnership more into our homes and our churches in these modern times, we must ask ourselves, *Can a church minister to the new diversities among families and still be a church? Can a church continue to be a church while ignoring changes in the family?* In times like these, all church members have to ask themselves, *What is acceptable and what is destructive? What is tolerable even though it is not ideal?*

Changes in family life have already had tremendous impact on churches. Two examples are single parents and working moms; they have revolutionized and diminished every church's voluntary workforce. Now there are more children to serve with fewer volunteers.

How does a church meet the challenges of this growing need? In the whole process of serving Christ during this confusing social revolution, our churches will be forced to evaluate modifications of traditional families and respond to the changes the way we think Christ would respond. These reevaluations are far reaching and will likely include issues such as priority of expenditures, the moral standing of unmarried couples living together, sermons about marriage when singles are present, urban churches serving children in poverty, cultural minorities, Christian grandparenting and unacceptable divorce.

Churches must face the fact that the Church—the family of God—is the only family many people will ever have.

More new questions keep coming: How can a church be redemptive without moral compromise? How can a church be forgiving without becoming permissive? What can be done to spark spiritual reformation in people who are caught up in moral despair? How much brokenness in people's past can a church accept while preaching a holistic gospel that keeps attracting hurting people like a holy magnet? And how willing is a church to go into the ghettos of society to rescue millions of hurting children?

After all these questions are answered, churches must face the fact that the Church—the family of God—is the only family many people will ever have. To be true to themselves, the Lord and their mission, our churches must go to work. We have a sacred responsibility to salt a decaying society with Christ's good news. And while we must be cautious about thinking a church can ever be a substitute for a biological family, that may be the best option for many of today's kids. Where churches can, they must strengthen the human family, but when the human family can't be strengthened, the family of God has to do what it can to fill the void. Children, regardless of the circumstances of their birth or their living conditions, must be shown in every possible way that Christ has a better way for them than they sometimes see at home.

THE POWER OF THE PARTNERSHIP

As we try to meet these needs, we must remember this partnership is a three-way alliance between the biological family, the church family and God—the heavenly Father. God is the senior member of this family partnership. In all our efforts in family and church, we depend on His enablement and grace to be what we can be and to become what He wants us to become.

If the task seems too large and even overwhelming, good. The empowering enablement to do something great for a child in the name of the Lord only comes to us after we have tried our best and asked God to do the rest. The enablement in the Early Church as recorded in Acts was like that—they were asked to do great things beyond all human ability. And when they gave their best in creativity, imagination and implementation, God came through time after time with miraculous resources. In its care for children, every church has to do much better, and it can because of the One who sends us.

Let's consider several ways God can strengthen the family and their church through this partnership.

This Partnership Can Validate Your Church's Purpose

Too many churches in North America have a foggy mission. Thousands of people meet at church each week to do what they have always done and go home satisfied that they have done their duty for another week. But in this frightening epidemic of children's problems, every church—whether in the country, town, suburbs or city—is touched by these concerns in some way. Ignoring them will not make them go away.

Offering ministry to people with needs is a common perspective for shaping ministry. It attracts both those who receive ministry and those who give ministry. By renewing our churches, we create a new vision, have a new impact on a community, and show a new concern for those in the fellowship who face these problems. We establish a new commitment to serve every family who is open to the gospel on the assumption that all parents have some concern about whether they are going to be able to effectively raise their children. For example, when parents hold their own newborn for the first time, they become aware of a responsibility that will not go away for at least 20 years, and will probably be with them all the days of their lives.

This idea of renewing a church or giving it higher visibility in the community shines through the story of a student pastor who went to a small Oregon coastal town to plant a church. He went there without one contact, only with the assurance from God that he was to go. For six months he worked as a bag boy in the only grocery store in town. By doing this he made contacts with many young families. Soon the pastor, his wife and their children started an after-school boys' and girls' club program on Tuesdays in their family room. The group grew, so they started a similar group on Monday. Then another group on Wednesday afternoon. Then another on Thursday and finally one on Friday.

By that time, they had enough family contacts to think about starting a church, so they did. About three years after the church was started, a reporter asked five or six families why they were a part of the new church that had no facilities, little money and no seasoned reputation. Almost in unison, they replied, "We're worried about our kids having right influences. When the new pastor showed our children love, it was natural to start loving him in return."

Could it be that serious commitments to children in every church would create a new curiosity about the Church and its potential importance in people's lives? A veteran country preacher used to tell beginning pastors, "When you care for the children, the whole extended family will show interest."

Even folks who say church is irrelevant, unconcerned with real issues, too self-serving or has nothing important to say to contemporary people are forced to listen when a church serves their children in the name of Christ.

This Partnership Can Provide Faith Resources for Parenting

Parenting is a task for which people have little training. It never fails that when I buy a car, the salesperson gives me more instructions about the automobile than anyone in our society gave me about parenting. To become whole persons, children need parents and other adults to feed them

Could it be that serious commitments to children in every church would create a new curiosity about the Church and its potential importance in people's lives?

faith. But what parent knows how to do that naturally?

A church can offer parenting training to parents. Sometimes this training is done in a formal class setting. Other times it happens when a faithful believer shares his own discoveries about Christian parenting. Many of us have learned a lot about parenting by teaching children's Sunday School classes. And more progressive churches are now distributing books and pamphlets about Christian parenting.

The following essay is a first-person account written by a young woman who was raised in a church I (Neil) once pastored. The essay is entitled "God Called (with a Little Help)" and demonstrates how vital it is for a church to help persons be good parents.

How does God decide whom to call to do ministry? I can't answer for the rest of you, but I know how my call came about. One day (well it wasn't exactly a day, since they don't measure time in heaven), one moment in eternity, God was looking down on our church and realized that we were going to need a new director of religious education soon. Don't ask me how God knew this, He just did. So God called His counselors together, and they started looking over potential candidates to be God-called to this ministry. This is where my mother comes in.

My mother joined God in heaven a little over three years ago, when God knew it was time for her reward and I didn't know how much I still needed her here on Earth. My mother was a reserved person and seldom stood up for herself or her needs. However, you could always count on my mother to stand up for her family.

My mother would never dream of considering herself one of God's counselors, but I imagine she did enjoy listening in on their discussions now and then, since she was a curious person who took pleasure in learning new things. It was part of her heritage as a schoolteacher for many years. As Mom was listening at this moment in eternity, she heard my name mentioned, so she moved in closer to listen better. Someone was talking about my qualifications as a potential religious education director, and without hesitation, my mother stood up for her daughter. She declared, "Call her; she knows the stories." "She knows the stories?" "Yes," replied my mother, "when you teach children about God's love, you must be able to tell them the stories. Jesus told stories. She knows the stories."

God must have chuckled at her insistence and maternal pride and asked Mom, "How can you be so sure she knows the stories?"

Her humble reply, "She knows the stories because I taught them to her."

I received the call, and I plan to fulfill it. Thanks, Mom, I love you.[4]

Every person who touched Wave Dreher or her mother, Bertha Beltz, had some small part in this faith development that moves across generations. Bertha learned the stories because someone told them to her in a church somewhere, and she sharpened the stories by telling them over and over to children in the churches where she taught Sunday School. And Bertha told them to her daughter at home.

Every church multiplies its impact on children when it gives parents training and resources for faith development at home.

This Partnership Can Build a Child's Spiritual Foundation
The community of faith has a great track record for changing people one at a time. Some of the most effective Christians are those who were loved to Christ by someone who did not worry about their home environment that could not be changed or about how sophisticated the local church's programs might or

might not be. Instead, these mentors simply loved a child and left the results with the Lord. They had the idea—do what we can do and trust God to do what we cannot do.

Sometimes a child feels loved as a result of the smallest things that we may not understand but feel God leading us to do. Dr. Miriam Hall—veteran teacher, former children's ministry denominational executive and seminary professor—told us David's story:

We must do what we can do and trust God to do what we cannot do.

She first met him in a Sunday School class when he was eight. In his class, he was a noticeable exception to the other children in his ragged jeans and scuffed tennis shoes. He was a handsome boy, but his smile was tentative and his eyes filled with pain. When he spoke, he stammered and said, "Me do it," like a child much younger than his eight years. One day, his Sunday School teacher called at David's home where he found half a dozen teens and young adults in an environment of unbelievable filth and an immoral atmosphere. While both parents worked, David and his numerous brothers were left in the questionable care of an assortment of young uncles—most of whom were more interested in beer and girlfriends than in caring for boys.

Later the teacher discovered that a tragic fire had occurred while the children were home alone. In the fire, a baby died, and David was labeled the culprit because he had been playing with matches.

The story continues—but gets better:

Several years later when David was older, one of my seminary students was his Sunday School teacher and I went to observe the teaching. To my delight, I also observed a very different David. Instead of a shy, withdrawn, stuttering child, I now saw a bright-eyed, happy-feeling boy doing a Bible memory activity with the other children. As the other children called out the words of the verse, he located the correct word cards and arranged them in the right order. His backward speech was gone; he spoke normally for a child his age.

A few moments later, a visitor entered the class to check on who wanted tickets for an upcoming Royals game. All over the class, eager children shared their excitement.

"My dad's taking me," said one. "I'm going with Dad and my uncle," chimed in another.

Something drew my attention to David. The light had gone out of his eyes and he hung his head. He had no one to take him. Slumped in his seat, he was once again the dejected boy of earlier days.

But his teacher quickly moved to David's side and put his arm around him. He spoke softly, but I could hear the words. "Don't worry, David. I'll get you a ticket and you can go to the game with me."

Instantly David's head raised again. The light returned to his eyes. Once again, he was a happy, confident boy because someone cared.[5]

Though no one can predict David's future, it is likely to be significantly better than it would have been had he not been introduced to that Sunday School class.

As we heard David's story, we felt we wanted to help that child. Though we are miles from David and will likely never meet him, our emotions are not too different from those of many caring adults. People just like us are in churches around the country, and they want to help, too. They may never be able to teach a Sunday School class or sing in the choir, but many will be willing to do something to help kids like David. They stand ready if we'll share the vision, the needs and the names of those who need help.

This Partnership Can Give People Opportunities to Influence Children's Lives

Too often in our stories of faith, we hear only of a Sunday School teacher or a Christian worker who dramatically affected a child for Christ. It seems that one person did a heroic act of faith that won the child and changed his or her life forever. In fact, most children who come to Christ are won through the influences of many different people. That's why we call the Church the community of faith and the family of God—it often involves the combined efforts of many.

Let's consider Tricia's story of faith told by a friend of children, Mrs. B. We need to think about how many people contributed to it. This event took place when Tricia was eight. In a church service, Tricia had asked Christ into her life, and a caring Sunday School teacher had instructed her that faith was to be shared and not hoarded.

So she shared her faith, and her friends made fun of her. Tricia told Mrs. B., "I don't want to be a Christian anymore." Puzzled, Mrs. B. asked the reason. "Because my

friends make fun of me. They think I am dumb to believe in Jesus, and they say bad words to me," Tricia
replied.

But after discussing
her feeling with Mrs. B.,
Tricia tried again. One day
when one of her friends let
fly a string of swear words,
Tricia said, "You shouldn't
say words like that."

Her friend replied, "I
know. I wish I could stop,
but I just can't."

"I know who can help
you stop," responded Tricia.
"I'll take you home and let
my mother tell you about
Christ." And that is what
she did.[6]

*The influence
of the home
environment and
relationships with
parents
cannot be
overestimated.*

We should think of all the people who did something to
influence Tricia and her friend.
There were parents. The family
of God helped them and gave them the resources to live out their
faith in their home before their children. Psychologists and edu-
cators tell us that the influence of the home environment and
relationships with parents cannot be overestimated.

Then let's consider committed children's leaders at church.
They spent hours preparing materials to teach, praying for children and visiting boys and girls in their homes.

Then there were the pastor and church lay leaders. The pastor even included times in the worship service when he shared

something special for children. He bent down to shake Tricia's hand and greet her personally as she left the church following the worship service. Along with the pastor, the lay leaders on the administrative team had a part in the congregation's commitments to make the church friendly to children.

And don't forget Mrs. B. How easy it would have been for her to react in shock when Tricia said she didn't want to be a Christian anymore. Instead, Mrs. B. heard the confusion behind those words and helped a child more clearly understand faith.

This Partnership Can Discover Benefits to Your Family and Church

There are many other benefits a ministry partnership between church and children provides. The following is a partial but exciting list of these benefits:

- Ministry to children makes a church relevant.
- Ministry to children helps society solve many of its problems. The generosity of American society to the needs of children has not solved those needs. New solutions are needed, and the raw materials for some solutions can be found only in a church.
- Ministry to children can be accomplished without increased spending or more red tape. A church is made up of people who are experienced at raising children and experienced in Christian service. What a magnificent army for changing the problems children face in so many places.
- Ministry to children can use every person in some way.
- Ministry to children provides Christian marriage and family models. Think of the impact on the nation if thousands of children could experience real-life examples of happily married Christian couples. One teenager

from a dysfunctional home was overheard to remark, "I didn't know people could have a happy family. The people at church have given me a goal for my life and marriage that I have never seen before."

A Testimony: How My Church Is Raising My Kids

When he heard about this book, Arnold Thomas, a member of my (Neil's) mentoring group, volunteered to tell how his church serves his family. Here's his moving first-person essay:

Ruby was the first. She worked in the nursery where we took Suzanne. They became good buddies. Even when Suzanne became a toddler and could have gone into the room with the bigger kids, she stayed with Ruby to take care of the "little babies."

When Suzanne became ill with leukemia, there were Ingrid and Denise. They took care of Suzanne sometimes. Or they would help her stressed-out parents. They occasionally went with Suzanne and her "mommy" to chemotherapy treatments. They were there when she died at age four and helped with the funeral. Bill prayed and fasted for Suzanne and us every Monday for a year before she died.

Seven-year-old Christy's buddies are Karen, the Sunday School superintendent's wife; Karen, the pastor's wife; and Miss Judy. Dick and Norma are "adopted" Grandma and Grandpa. And there are "cousins" Melissa, Anthony, Jeremy and Baby Austin.

Audrey, at 11, is our oldest. She has a boyfriend, Jim, who isn't a boyfriend; they're "just friends." Joe and

Janet are doing such a great job raising Jim and his brother, Toby. My wife, Mary, and I are pleased that Audrey has the opportunity to experience such a healthy relationship at an early age. Monique is Audrey's "older sister."

This is an example of how our church family empowers our biological family. We are related by rebirth rather than by natural birth. We are not blood relatives but relatives by the adoptive family bond Christ provides. We have aunts, uncles, fathers, mothers, brothers, sisters and cousins, just like Jesus promised. They are examples—whether good, bad or mediocre—for my kids to live by. They love my kids and then give them back when they've had enough.

The church is helping us raise our kids, and I am grateful. The government cannot raise my children. It is too powerful, awkward and dangerous. My town cannot raise my children. Neighbors are transient, aloof and wary. Our family—the church—knows us, loves us and treats us as kin.

Here's the secret of all this. Governments, communities, churches or cultures can only adequately impact or raise children to the extent that they assume and communicate the characteristics of a family. The family relationships of our churches—just being there intimately, lovingly and consistently—are what make kids grow spiritually.

PART 3

BUILDERS OF FUTURE GENERATIONS

We pray for children
who worry about being too fat, too skinny,
too old or too young,
who almost made the honor roll,
who are nurtured by a Sunday School teacher
and loved by their church;

and we pray for children
who are dying for love and attention,
who never had a kite, an allowance or an adult friend,
who have no one to say "You're great"
and "You can do it!"

IT'S HARD TO FORGET A LOVING CHURCH

Tribute to the Folks on Dubay Street

Long before Detroit became a jungle of urban blight, members of a small congregation on the east side of the city were the living the gospel by loving children. They were living examples of Jesus' teaching about salt and light. Although more than 2 million lived in the city at that time, the little church on Dubay Street was an island of faith made up mostly of people who had migrated to the city to work in the automobile industry. Most of those who attended the church lived within a three-mile radius of their meeting place.

The Dubay Church originated with Betsy Healy and Sophia Hoffler, who began Sunday-afternoon Bible classes in their living rooms. As attendance grew, they held classes in every room of their houses, and some classes met on their front porches and under trees.

No one knows for sure whether the founders ever thought about whether the Sunday School might become a church. However, when their homes could no longer accommodate the children in Sunday School, they established a church.

During those early years my (Neil's) father began attending the Sunday School regularly when he was 12. Seven years later he was married. He and his wife attended the church and took me there when I was two weeks old. The teachers at the church were already his best adult friends. Today, we might call those teachers faith mentors. Although they had no name for what they did, they loved kids and showed it.

To catch the details of our tribute to the folks on Dubay Street, read the following conversation.

H. B.: Tell me about the facilities of the Dubay Church.

Neil: To a child who was first taken to the church at two weeks of age, the facilities seemed large. But memory has a way of making things bigger and better than they really were. The church was, in fact, a cement-block row house crowded into the middle of a city block. The entire first floor, along with an overflow porch, was used as a sanctuary. As needed, the worship area was divided with curtains that looked like bedsheets into spaces for youth and adult Sunday School classes. Those same white sheets also were used for stage curtains for Christmas and Easter pageants. The pageants had angels dressed in homemade white garments with glittering cardboard wings, and Christmas shepherds were always dressed in borrowed oversized wool bathrobes.

H. B.: Tell me about the people who attended the house church on Dubay and about the church leaders.

Neil: Everyone knew everyone. All were expected to attend every service. If you were absent, someone checked following the service to be sure you were not ill or losing interest. It was informal accountability, but no one knew to call it that. For them it was friends caring for friends, just as Jesus would.

The lay leaders had places of elected responsibility, but they were like people who pass out presents at birthday parties—the titles and elections to office were no big deal. We were family—God's family—so all worked together. We took turns furnishing the coal from our own basements one winter so that the church could have heat.

We were a big happy family. We knew everybody's business and everyone knew ours. Most of the children attended the same schools. Sometimes old-fashioned family fights took place, too.

We are family— God's family—so we must all work together.

When death took one of our number, we used Miller's Funeral Home, bought funeral wreaths from Van Maele's Florists and buried our dead at Forest Lawn cemetery just across the fence from Lynch School.

Lay leaders were a lot like heads of clans; they led because somebody had to do it, and because the church family wanted them to do it. It was like stepping forward and offering to do some function or service, just as an older brother often does in extended families.

H. B.: Who were the pastors that impacted your faith development as a child?

Neil: Two stand out even now—Patience Hole and Robert North. I love the memory of Pastor Patience Hole. A mother in Zion to us, she was a woman about 10 years older than my parents who loved us into faith and grace. She expected us to be good Christians, so we stretched to what she expected. She thought we could be spiritually strong, so we became more like Christ.

Pastor Hole, along with her husband—a produce peddler who ran his business from the back of his truck—and her little girl, lived in a basement apartment in the church on Dubay Street. Although Pastor Hole was a competent person, her love and simple piety influenced us most. She cared for the spiritual needs of her flock like a loving mother cares for her newborn baby. No need for her to worry about women's liberation issues; she was pastor and spiritual leader because of who she was in her relationship to Christ and to us.

The congregation loved her because she touched our lives with the gospel. She lived the Christ-filled life before us. Like Jesus in the Incarnation, she identified with us in every possible way, and she was a part of our lives at births, deaths, Holy Communion, baptisms, job losses and health problems. The small resources of money and limited facilities of the church didn't keep her from leading the family of God to care for each other and to share their faith with other children in the neighborhood.

Without getting overly emotional about the relationship, she was an example of what the writer of Hebrews spoke about, "of whom the world was not worthy" (Heb. 11:38, *NKJV*). By her life, she taught us devotion, acceptance, compassion, faithfulness and authenticity. I often chuckle when I think about her name because she really needed patience to lead that little company of believers.

H. B.: Who was the second leader?

Neil: A self-made pastor, Robert North, arrived when I was in my early teen years. The church had grown some and had moved to a converted bank building on the corner of Van Dyke and Knodell. In those days, such a building was easy to purchase because it had failed as a bank during the Great Depression and now had limited use. I remember working with the men of the church to tear out the old bank vault so that we could have space for worship.

H. B.: Earlier you called him a self-made man. What does that mean?

Neil: I mean he had no opportunities for formal education, so he educated himself. He studied hard, observed life and trained himself to be an effective, loving pastor. Being a pastor was really a second career for him. He quit his job at the factory to become a minister.

No one knows how he could afford to serve our church with a family of five children. It's still a mystery. But he did. His family was an important part of the church to the other families. So his wife and children were heart-deep involved in most events. Church choir, picnics in the park, social gatherings following funerals, church sports, revival meetings, worship at church, Sunday School classes, Christmas programs, prayer meetings—almost anything you can think of that could be done at church was part of their family agenda. Five children meant that nearly every Sunday School class had one of their children in the class. The family modeled what a home centered on Christ could be like. In many ways, their family taught us as much about Christ as did their father's preaching.

Pastor North taught us liberality, steadfastness, trust and faith. In this close-knit community of faith, we learned to face life and accept death. We learned to love troubled people, rehabilitate dysfunctional families, provide food for needy people, serve homeless people in the city's rescue missions, care for one another in bad economic times, cherish children as the hope of the future and nurse spiritually battered people back to wholeness. I love to think of those times as a beautiful human mosaic of service to others.

H. B.: It sounds almost too idealistic, something like a church for the Cleavers in a time and place when everything was right.

Neil: Sorry to leave that impression. Times have changed. I know we can't re-create those former days. I don't want to. Our situation was far from ideal. Our people had frequent layoffs with no public assistance. Coming out of the Great Depression, many of our people worked for the WPA, a government work program. Then came World War II when housewives left their homes for work and young men went away to fight a war. One of our number was killed in action.

Sometimes, it seemed everyone in our church was in crisis because we made everyone's problems our own. We prayed for one another. We supported one another spiritually, emotionally and sometimes economically. Perhaps the church was so influential in our lives because circumstances were bad.

H. B.: What ministry or program shaped you the most?

Neil: As I think about it, I know it was not the programs of the church that shaped me. It was the people. And they were not perfect or special or wonderfully gifted. Sometimes they were not any of those. They simply attempted to live out the teachings of Jesus in their relationships with one another, and generally they succeeded. When people fell, as they sometimes did, the community of faith gathered around them, loved them, offered them a lift and urged them to try again. Often we saw grace most at work in the incredible imperfections of people.

H. B.: Were new children and their families welcomed there?

Neil: Oh, yes. During my childhood years in that church, I learned the Church is one of the few places where troubled, even dysfunctional, families can find help and healing. I'm convinced many dysfunctional families are attracted to a caring church just because they have never experienced an extended family that would love them regardless of what they have done or who they are. It is unconditional love—what theologians call agape love.

Think about it. Many social problems faced by society have some solution in the Church. Such accepting love cannot be found anywhere else in our society. Of course, not all churches provide an ideal sense of extended family, but a church can and it should. God expects it and even provides the enablement to make it possible. It is a spirit and priority and way of life as much as a method or strategy. For 2,000 years, the love of Christ has motivated and energized people to care for children. It still works today. And when they experience it, children and their parents treasure that love.

H. B.: I'm nervous about what sounds too good to be true. How can a church touch an individual child when the contemporary agenda in many churches seems to be building bigger buildings, developing more programs and being a religious business rather than an extended spiritual family?

Neil: My tribute to the Dubay folks is intended to help readers realize ministry to a child may involve programs, buildings, big budgets and large staffs. But it also can be the work of ordinary people in small, out-of-the-way places. Although I can't prove it, I suspect that most Christian leaders came from such a setting.

Serving and loving one child may even impact the future of the nation and shape generations yet unborn.

Serving and loving one child may even impact the future of the nation and shape generations yet unborn. Today in every church you will find children who will tomorrow head families, be community leaders and work in secular settings that desperately need the influence of Christ. Right now in some churches, there is a future Mother Teresa, a future Chuck Colson, a future James Dobson or a future ordinary Joe.

Think, too, about children who need what the Church offers but who never experience it. Without the influence of Christ, potential killers and shocking social misfits live down the street or around the corner from many churches. Like children everywhere, these people offer us a narrow window of opportunity in which to introduce them to Christ so that they can learn about the most wonderful way to live that has ever been discovered.

H. B.: Can you tell me specifically what the little house church on Detroit's Dubay Street did for you? Is there something reproducible that every church can do for its children, regardless of the church's size, location or doctrine?

Neil: Let me offer a quick list of things any church can do without spending a dollar:

- Love children and let them know it.
- Introduce children to Jesus as their friend.
- Give time to children and become their adult friend.
- Don't wait until everything is perfect to start.
- Understand that children will be forgiving of mistakes.
- Work with confidence, knowing that faith is caught as well as taught.
- Teach parents that children's faith development is as important as good nutrition.
- Be quick to show the compassion of Christ to children who are in family crises. You may be their only hope.

H. B.: Before we finish, I suppose you want to tell your story about how my Sunday School evangelist grandfather impacted your life.

Neil: I was afraid you would never ask. I joke lots of times that your grandfather almost ruined my faith. But before I tell my story, why not introduce your grandfather to our readers? He knew the awesome, eternal value of touching children with the love of Christ.

H. B.: My grandfather was a Sunday School evangelist who traveled from church to church, helping congregations double the size of their Sunday School attendance over a two- or three-week period. His strategy was to preach inspirationally to the people and then organize them for a big Sunday School rally on the last Sunday of the revival.

The process was to increase the church's impact on families in the community, starting with those who lived nearest to the church. Usually, the campaign lasted for three Sundays, and church services were held each night of the week. In those days, guest preachers usually stayed in people's homes. So evangelists and church members sometimes became well acquainted over a two-week period.

Granddad's goal was to help a church see and respond to its potential, which included children. He believed a combination of organization, hard work and inspiration would draw new people into the church. He and Grandmother sang together in revivals. So the music, his inspirational preaching and his practical plan made him effective. In many places, the churches actually doubled their Sunday School attendance for the closing Sunday School rally. Can you imagine the excitement that caused? His ministry fit his times exactly, and he had a full schedule. For many years, I often heard people say, "We had our largest Sunday School attendance ever when Dr. A. S. London was here as our evangelist."

Neil: That's a great introduction, almost too lofty for my story. But I still love to tell it.

At the little house church on Dubay Street, your grandfather came as evangelist when Pastor Patience Hole was our minister. The incident took place on a dark, cold Michigan November night, a night when only the faithful would consider attending church. The crowd was down, and your grandfather was trying to impress his hearers with the Kingdom value of every child.

I was four years old and sound asleep during most of the service—that is, until he woke me. In a moment of inspiration, your grandfather grabbed me, held me high over his shoulder and shouted at the top of his voice, "How much is this boy worth?" It was a hard, demanding question to ask anyone, and he knew it.

But can you imagine what that did to me—an unforgettable question comes booming into your consciousness when you are a sleepy four-year-old? I felt as though I was in the midst of a thousand nightmares combined. I love to remind you, H. B., that your grandfather almost ruined my faith, and who knows how much he damaged my psyche that night.

However, A. S. London's intention when he used me as a living illustration for his sermon is exactly what we mean when we say it takes a church to really rear a child.

Dr. London's question still rings in my ears. His question still makes me think about my relationship to children. His question makes me look at children in church and department stores and playgrounds and parks. His question makes me wonder about the potential of every child I meet.

IT IS IMPORTANT TO RECOGNIZE CHILDHOOD JOYS

"I have tried, but I can't forget you," a 41-year-old scientist wrote to the pastor of a small country church. "My mind keeps going back to our years together." The writer, who was experiencing a midlife crisis, told the pastor about how he had sought fulfillment on the dead-end streets named position, prestige and power. Now, the scientist had come full circle and was reaching out to people who had nourished his faith in his childhood. In his letter he inquired about former Sunday School teachers and childhood church chums.

Pastor Jim read the section from the letter where the scientist got to the heart of the matter to a group of Sunday School teachers: "I've gained professional success—more than I could have imagined. But I feel an emptiness at the center of myself. I am on a journey back to God, and my childhood memories are giving me many needed signposts. I can't get away from what the church meant to me then."

The scientist's letter sounds like this adage: You can take a child out of the country, but you can't take the country out of a child. Novels, movies, TV sitcoms and talk shows work hard to keep childhood traumas churning in our minds. It has become a cultural addiction to discuss dysfunctional problems from childhood on afternoon TV shows. Many people blame their parents for ruining their lives.

But isn't there another side? What about the positive Christian influences that came to us through a church? What about all those times when a Sunday School teacher showed us love, when a scout leader answered our tough questions about God and when other caring folks supported us through a crisis? Maybe it's time to downplay our scars and to take an encouraging inventory of the more nourishing experiences.

JESUS USES HOMECOMINGS TO TEACH

Jesus riveted truth in His hearers' minds with unforgettable stories called parables. That's what He did when the Pharisees groused about His "terrible" offense of eating with tax collectors and "sinners." Instead of defending Himself, Jesus told three stories, which can be found in Luke 15. One story was about a lost son and his stay-at-home brother.

The story about the two sons highlights the father's relationship with them. It emphasizes the warmth of home, strength of family affection and shared inheritances. It also shows what children will remember for a lifetime. Nowhere in all of literature can one find a more heartwarming example of what God means for the Church to be than the father's love at the prodigal's homecoming.

Love permeates the story. Unconditional acceptance is the order of the day. Celebration of renewed relationships crackles from every detail in the passage.

Think again about the younger brother, often called the prodigal. He had a consuming passion to experience the outside world. He wanted freedom to live his own way. He even expected his father to finance his folly. And that's what the father did, without even a mild protest.

Every father and son can identify in some measure with the parable. It is the age-old struggle of when to go and when to stay. However, Jesus does not forget to tell about the self-righteous stay-at-home son who obviously represented the Pharisees to whom our Lord was speaking. A convincing argument can be made for comparing the stay-at-home son with contemporary church members who complain.

Several Bible commentators suggest everyone is represented in the story, either as the prodigal son or as the stay-at-home son. The father represents God, who loves all of us with an everlasting love, despite our sins or the consequences of our bad choices. However, to consider the Church's task of shaping children into Christlikeness, let's look at the story through a rather unusual lens. Try to see the parable as a description of an unforgettable memory of God's gracious care for you.

Although the wandering boy traveled miles from home, he never could shake his father from his memory. As he started toward the alluring city, his newly accepted value system played tricks on him. So even early in his waywardness he was forced to compare home with what he thought he would enjoy in the new setting.

A rude awakening soon came, however. Even at the zenith of his far-country merriment, he felt a strong twinge of homesickness. When he came to his senses while feeding pigs, he remembered how well even hired hands ate at his father's table while he was now starving to death. Then he reasoned, *I've made a stupid mistake.* So he started home, practicing his repentance speech as he walked: "I have sinned against heaven and against you. I am no longer worthy to be called your son; make me like one of your hired men" (Luke 15:18-19, *NIV*).

REAL LOVE IS HARD TO FORGET

Regret and forgiveness, dread and welcome, selfishness and generosity, and realism and tenderness saturate the story. Much to the prodigal's surprise, the father treated him as if he had never left home. Even when the elder son experienced ugly rage, the father showed agape affection.

What unmerited favor the father showed both boys. To the prodigal son, the father said, "My son was lost and is found. He was dead and is alive" (see v. 32) After reading that passage, a country preacher remarked that it was real good news.

To the stay-at-home son, the father said, "Everything I have is yours" (Luke 15:31, *NIV*). Of those words, the preacher said that that's about as good as you can get.

KIDS CAN'T ESCAPE MEMORIES

There's an important message in this story for the family of God. As a church stimulates faith development in children, the family of God must remember that kids never escape the Father's influence. Having tasted God's nearness and having received love from the Church, sons and daughters can't lose that either.

Such memories are like a brand on the soul. Everything the Church invests in a child continues to be played over and over for years in the adult's mind: *How can I ever forget that a group of believers once loved me?* Once someone told me to use the parable's language—I could come back to the Father's house safe and sound.

The parable and its meaning are good news to all of us who take our spiritual responsibility to children seriously. Wherever the child goes, we go. Whatever the kid does, we do. Whomever the child associates with, we are there. Regardless of the intensity and depth of misery—even to feeding pigs or experiencing physical hunger—we are there, pointing the child home to God. Memory follows the wanderers down every rebellious mile and stalks them down every spiritual detour.

THE GOSPEL HELPS SEEDS TO TAKE ROOT

That may be what the Bible means when it advises us to train up a child in the way he or she should go (see Prov. 22:6). One rebellious 41-year-old woman said, "I just couldn't get away from the love of the Church though I lived 2,000 miles away in geography and 25 years away from my childhood." The Church's influence is astonishing. Count on it.

Of course, many who reject God's reign like to recount unhappy church experiences. Admittedly, there are too many heartbreaking examples of mistreatment, but such mistreatment is not genuine Christianity. Whether we are discussing dollars, diamonds or churches, rejecting the authentic because we have been fooled by the counterfeit is self-defeating and shortsighted.

WE CAN CREATE UNFORGETTABLE MEMORIES FOR CHILDREN

Many of us remember what the Church taught us in child-hood—so much of what we learn as kids we never forget.

Whether or not we learned these truths as children or as adults, we are obligated to pass them on to future generations. Here's a list of the basics we must share with our kids.

Responding with a Simple Faith

I (Neil) was wonderfully drawn to the Savior when an invitation was given in a regular service. Although the minister's invitation was primarily directed to adults, children were not excluded. When I responded, my Sunday School teacher introduced me to a simple faith in Christ. She told me about Jesus, the friend of children. She spoke of a God of acceptance, love and understanding who knew me better than I knew myself.

Many of us remember what the Church taught us in childhood—so much of what we learn as kids we never forget.

Maybe what I felt then is what Jesus meant when He said, "Unless you are converted and become as little children, you will by no means enter the kingdom of heaven" (Matt. 18:3, *NKJV*). These remembrances make me feel close to my spiritual roots planted by that little church of my childhood.

Facing Death

My parents lost a full-term baby girl at birth, probably because of incompetent medical care. I (Neil) was an only child, a 10-year-old. I remember that troubling time, and I wondered where God was. It was a critical moment for my faith development. I had no idea how to deal with death. I could not comprehend the loss of a baby. Members of our extended biological family did everything they could do. All of the funeral customs of our culture were faithfully followed. But what I remember most was the family of God showing us love, and I remember how they spoke with assurance about the resurrection of Jesus, which makes us victors over our fear of the grave. Even more, I remember their visiting our home, their hugging me, their talking to me and their praying with me.

Living Faith in Relationships

The core of Christianity, according to Christ, is to love the Lord with the whole self and to love our neighbors as ourselves (see Matt. 22:37-49). That is a big order that requires hard work and divine enablement. The first-century disciples demonstrated this love of neighbors so well. This love in a church is like love in a family that can be communicated through loving deeds without saying a single word. Living in love among the people of God is sometimes tough, requiring high standards of behavior and authentic accountability.

Once our little church had an awful fuss. Hot words burned and bruised. Our family decided we would move to a nearby congregation to find peace and harmony. On Sunday morning, as we left home for church, my father turned the car toward the old church rather than the new one. My mother was puzzled, and asked, "Where are you going? I thought we were going to a new church today." My dad replied, "I can't do it. We'll have to find a way to work it out." As a Christian under construction, about 12 years old, I learned a lot from that incident.

Serving Others

Once a month a church in greater Los Angeles takes a group of 9- to 11-year-olds to serve food to homeless people at the Los Angeles Mission. I once watched them serve an evening meal. Homeless people reached out to the kids, who beamed with pride. Everyone gained something wonderful in that relationship.

Performing acts of service in Jesus' name helps children form a cornerstone for a life of meaning—fulfillment in life is multiplied by serving others. Robert Coles, a Harvard research psychiatrist who studies the spirituality of children, tells about a young African-American college student who put himself at risk as a civil rights activist. Later, Coles asked the student, "Why do you keep at this, given the danger and the obstacles?" The student gave this surprising answer, "The satisfaction, man, the satisfaction."[1] That's a lesson to learn in church.

Belonging

The traditions of the Church help children feel they belong and produce predictability in a time of rapid change. In *Fiddler on the Roof*, the main character Tevye says: "Because of our traditions, everyone knows who he is and what God expects him to do."[2]

In the church of my childhood, we had many traditions: Christmas caroling that included people of every age, watchnight services on New Year's Eve to commit to making the New Year Christ centered, Easter sunrise services to celebrate the Resurrection, and Easter and Christmas programs with memorized recitations by every child.

Traditions put children in touch with the past even as they observe contemporary role models of the Christian faith. Rituals and ceremonies help kids feel connected to their own families at church, as well as to the historic Church, and provide them opportunities to participate.

OUR PERSONAL GROWTH POINTS SHAPE US

Each of us has a favorite way of remembering how we have been shaped by a church. Which of the values we received from church can we pass on? What new values should be added? What will we contribute to members of the next generation that they will feel obligated to share with the following generation?

Let's influence children so that they never get the Father and the Church out of their minds and hearts. Then they will be spoiled forever—unable to enjoy life apart from God—and they will point their children and grandchildren to Christ.

We pray for children
who love to wear the outlandish clothes their schoolmates are
wearing,
who forget their lunch money and their school assignments,
who fret about sitting on the bench at Little League games;

and we pray for children
who give birth to other children,
who fear their school will have a shooting like Columbine's,
who have never heard about the love of Jesus.

CHAPTER 10

CHRIST-CENTERED MARRIAGES HELP KIDS GROW

Making Home a Training Camp for Children

We've heard the advice: The best thing a parent can do for a child is to love the other parent. For our purpose, the idea should be altered a bit: The best thing a Christian couple can do for their kids is to strengthen their marriage in every way possible. The goal is to make every Christian marriage a training camp for the children from that marriage and to provide a model for every child who observes them from outside the family.

If the cornerstone of this book—it takes a Christ-centered church to rear strong, healthy kids—is right, then a church must do everything it can to build strong marriages and to help people create happy homes. Because a desire for a strong Christ-centered marriage is more often caught than taught, a church must be a garden of healthy family relationships. Many children will never experience anything faintly resembling a strong marriage or a happy Christian home unless they see it in families at church.

While building marriages may not be a church's only priority, every Christian leader must consider one marriage-ministry specialist's observation: "The heart of family ministry is the nature of the church, not merely its work."[1] Serving people and helping them develop healthy Christian relationships at home stands at the heart of a church's work. For that reason, discussion of ministry to children must include a discussion of how to make marriages work better.

DIVORCE RATES ARE ASTRONOMICAL

The United States has the highest divorce rate in the world.[2] About half of all marriages are expected to end in divorce within seven years.[3] Today, about 25 million fathers will not see their children during the year.[4] Half of single moms have been divorced. Most of the other single moms have never been married.[5]

So what chance do we have to save the children if the family is not healthy?

The answer rests in viewing marriage as God intended it to be and in enjoying the benefits of living in a healthy, loving family that is modeled after Christ and is nurtured by the Church.

Unfortunately, several decades ago, marriage, the most basic and universal of all human relationships, found itself under attack. The value of marriage was questioned and monogamy was debated as a result of such societal changes as readily accessible birth control, women's liberation, ease of divorce, freedom to be happy at any cost, increased cohabitation, and a rise in the number of unwed mothers and absentee fathers.

MARRIAGE IS GOOD FOR US AND FOR THE CHILDREN IN OUR LIVES

There seems to be at least a glimmer of good news. Marriage is receiving better reviews these days. For example, the book *The Case for Marriage* offers credible and convincing research that supports the premise that marriage is good for us. The data gathered by Linda J. Waite and Maggie Gallagher for their book shows that married people live longer, experience more happiness, are better off financially and enjoy better mental health. Many different studies are cited. The research is thorough and convincing. [6]

About the time the book was being published, Maggie Gallagher wrote an essay, "Why Marriage Is Good for You," which was published in the *City Journal of Manhattan*.[7] She opened a stimulating, hopeful essay by reporting how impressed she was with the scientific evidence that Waite presented to her.

As if addressing several of the main issues of this book, she writes:

> When Americans debate the value of marriage, most attention focuses on the potential harm to children of divorce or illegitimacy, and for good reason. Mountains of research tell us that children reared outside of intact marriages are much more likely than other kids to slip into poverty, become victims of child abuse, fail at school and drop out, use illegal drugs, launch into premature sexual activity, become unwed teen mothers, divorce, commit suicide and experience other signs of mental illness, become physically ill and commit crimes and go to jail. Yes, marriage protects children.[8]

Gallagher then uses David Letterman's top-10-style list to explain why marriage is good for us:

10. It's safer. Marriage lowers the risk that men and women will become victims of violence, including domestic violence.

9. It can save your life. Married people live longer and healthier lives.

8. It can save your kid's life. Children lead healthier, longer lives if parents get and stay married.

7. You will earn more money.

6. Married people not only make more money, they manage money better and build more wealth together than either would alone. You will manage money better. The longer you are married the more assets you acquire.

5. You'll tame his cheatin' heart (hers, too). Marriage increases sexual fidelity.

4. You won't go bonkers. Marriage is good for your mental health.

3. It will make you happy. For most people, the joys of the single life and of divorce are overrated.

2. Your children will love you more. Divorce weakens the bonds between parents and children over the long run.

1. You'll have better sex, more often . . . husbands and wives are more likely to report that they have an extremely satisfying sex life than are singles or cohabitors.[9]

That list of strengths is impressive, and those strengths are well worth having.

SUBSTITUTES FOR OLD-FASHIONED VALUES HAVE TURNED INTO SPIRITUAL SUICIDES

It seems clear now. Many current models of secularized family and marriage simply don't work. Living together, single parenthood, no-fault divorce, equal custody and many other so-called liberated practices—you name it—do not make good on their promises. Thousands seem to be asking, Did we give up too much? Maybe wandering off course from the old-fashioned idea that marriage and family and home are solid-rock anchors for life was emotional and spiritual suicide.

Could it be that hurting kids could help us get our perspective clear and focus our moral compass on Jesus?

Maybe while trying to give children what money can't buy, we develop a new appreciation for old values that produce new satisfactions. Could it be that thousands have had their fill of empty marriages and treadmill families? Maybe it's time to take our clue from the beautiful child who loved her teacher "two valentines' worth." Or maybe 10 or 20 valentines' worth.

Could it be that hurting kids could help us get our perspective clear and focus our moral compass on Jesus?

MARRIAGE CONFLICT IS REAL

During a sermon a fresh-from-seminary pastor said that genuinely Christian couples will never have problems getting along with each other. Because he was inexperienced and had never been married, members of the congregation overlooked his comment. Unfortunately, the pastor's view represents a common, inaccurate notion about marriage, family and child rearing.

Those of us who are married will acknowledge that we often have gigantic disagreements in our most important relationships simply because we are human. Even though we are serious followers of Christ, we still may be imperfect while interacting with the most important people in our lives. C. S. Lewis enjoyed telling about two people who quarreled so often as children and as teenagers that they married so they could quarrel "more conveniently."[10]

Conflicts occur in the best of marriages. The secret of a good marriage, however, is to learn to apply faith to the conflicts and continually ask how Christ wants us to behave. That is why we need the help of our churches. And using Christian resources like mercy, forgiveness and grace to solve the conflicts makes life better for us and provides a strong model for the next generation.

MARRIAGE IS HERE TO STAY

"Divorced" is the fastest-growing marital status category. The dramatic increase in divorces has shaken young people's confidence in marriage and has damaged many children. Many young people express skepticism in regard to marriage because they doubt that people can get along well enough to commit to spend a lifetime together. Interestingly, these are impressions of kids who observe the marriages of parents and friends.

Yet marriage is here to stay, and it often starts with a church wedding. Because as many as 75 to 80 percent of all marriages are solemnized by the Church, America's clergy continue to have at least some access to most couples. As we talk to people we meet along the way, we find that nearly all of them would marry the same person again, and even those who have been divorced plan to marry again.

In a George Barna survey, when asked the question, Did God intend for people to get married and stay in that relationship for life? 80 percent of married persons answered yes, and 76 percent of divorced persons said yes.[11] Apparently, marriage is here to stay. Now, we have to figure out how to make marriages stronger so that they thrive for a lifetime.

FAMILY TIES STRENGTHEN MARRIAGES

Let's consider five family ties that couples can use to strengthen their marriage. These same essentials can be used in training sessions in the congregation. For the development of boys and girls, parents in the Church should widely practice and share these ideas. Children need to learn about these ties so that they can begin forming ideas about their own future marriage. Without powerful shaping influences from the Church and from families in the community of faith, our kids are likely to repeat the same mistakes their parents made, which will continue or even increase the generational downward spiral.

Family Tie 1: Be Willing to Give
The prospects of having a healthy marriage are not good unless both partners give themselves wholly to the relationship. Every marriage demands self-giving love. Each partner has to give a lot, or the marriage will flounder. The liberating discovery occurs, however, when we think of the beautiful prayer of Saint Francis of Assisi, "For it is in giving that we receive."[12]

When we really love our spouses, we must be willing to accept our partner. A country preacher wisely advised members of the congregation to give what you are before you try to give what you have. Solid marriages are built on giving ourselves—soul, heart and body—to our spouse.

Although our partner may change throughout the years of marriage, he or she should never be our remodeling project. I (H. B.) love the threefold possibility in Dr. Richard Kremler's words: "Important factors leading to fragmentation of the home are a result of loss of understanding, giving up too soon and unreasonable expectations."[13]

Let's make the idea more positive by rephrasing his comment: We can have a strong, satisfying marriage by cultivating understanding, by dogged determination and by keeping our expectations realistic.

In building a strong marriage and a happy family, we must ask ourselves the following questions:

1. Are my expectations realistic?
2. Is there something happening in my mate's life that explains his or her behavior?
3. Am I willing to listen when my spouse has problems?

Issues outside the home may complicate our spouse's life. Our being aware of those possibilities helps. A woman said of her long-term marriage, "We have built a terrific relationship, not because we were instantly compatible, but because we were intensely committed."[14]

Most of these same questions can also be applied to parent-child awareness and relationships. Consider what takes place when Tim wants to play basketball more than anything else in the world. He tries out for the team, makes the first and second cut and then finds there are not enough uniforms for every player. He is not chosen for the team. He comes homes glum, goes to his room, slams the door and thinks life has ended.

The unthinking father goes to Tim's room and says, "Son, we don't act that way around here. Straighten up. Basketball's not the biggest thing in the world, and you should know that." But to Tim, basketball is the most important thing in his world. That is why he is heartbroken, but he also is hurt because no one seems to understand.

How much better for the father to go upstairs, knock on the door and ask Tim if he can enter the room. Then the father sits on the bed and is quiet for a moment. He says, "Tim, I probably never told you before, but I was cut from the team once. I don't know all you are feeling, but I know a little bit about how it hurts. Why don't we start playing hoops together? Then you can try again next year. I want you to know, Son, how proud I am of you. Now, let's go eat supper. Your mother and I would like for you to join us. We love you, Son."

Family Tie 2: Speak the Truth in Love and Ask Big Questions
Caring deeply for another person means we give other family members the right to express their opinions and give them space to develop their uniqueness. This right does not prohibit us as parents from setting standards for family behavior, but it teaches children how to state their opinions, how to consider consequences and how to be loving even to people who disagree with them.

Somewhere we heard about a woman in marriage counseling who said of her husband, "Oh, I believe he has a right to his own opinion; I just don't want to hear it." That's a common problem in many marriages. In a world of conflict, we need to give family members the right to speak their opinions. In this process, kids learn about love, acceptance and belonging. And children from dysfunctional homes whom we adopt at church also will be affected by this policy of freedom to speak when they see it in action in our families.

Ephesians 4:15 instructs us to speak the truth in love. Among other things, that means we will speak up when we see others about to engage in destructive behavior, negative habits or harmful attitudes. For too long we Christians have believed that keeping quiet—minding our own business, it is called—was the only way we could keep our speech holy and influential. We must seek to help people we love in the family and in the community of faith avoid the consequences of harmful actions and self-induced difficulties.

How is that done? By speaking the truth in love—making every effort to assess the reason for the problem and coming to a helpful conclusion.

One effective Christian counselor once told me (H. B.), "Every marriage or family problem I see is a result of people asking no questions or small questions." We should think of the implications of that statement. What are the big questions? Here are several for openers:

1. Why is this happening?
2. Why are we feeling pain?
3. Why are we irritable and moody?
4. Why are we silent?

The second set of questions is personal and more directed to our own behavior. These questions help us open up new possibilities of self-understanding:

1. How has my behavior or attitude contributed to this misunderstanding?
2. Have I been selfish?
3. Am I insensitive?
4. How have I been irresponsible?
5. Have I been stubborn?

The third set of questions relates to applying faith to the details of our marriage or in our relationships to children. The following questions bring the Bible and our relationship to Christ into the conflict, and that can be either soothing or convicting:

1. Are my faith and my handling of this situation consistent?
2. Am I practicing my faith in this situation?
3. What would Jesus do in this relationship?
4. Are my behavior and attitude pleasing to God?
5. Could I live with my spouse and children in the future acting the way I do in our relationships now?
6. What am I doing in this conflict that would make the people I most love become more like Christ?

To build Christ-exalting marriages and families, we must be willing to ask the big questions, to speak the truth in love and to use the truth we discover to change our conduct into living that honors Christ.

This principle played out in the life of a boy named Kevin. After months of senseless teen rebellion, Kevin was influenced by a youth pastor who practiced tough love. The youth pastor refused to allow Kevin to get by with actions or attitudes that were detrimental to his emotional, physical or spiritual well-being. In trying to explain the relationship, Kevin told his mother, "Mom, this guy really does love me." Kevin's mother, threatened by this new person in her son's life, said, "I love you, too, Son. You know that. I love you very much." Kevin replied, "Yes, Mom, I know. But he tries to understand the way I think. He accepts me in spite of my faults. And he doesn't take any excuses from me."

Love is necessary, but it is not enough. To have strong marriages and healthy families, we must be bold and brave enough to ask the big questions, so we can understand the other person's behavior, so we can put ourselves in another person's position, so we can understand our own behavior and so we can personally change at the precise points where change is most needed.

Asking and answering these tough questions help us get to the main point of what troubles our relationships and help us avoid blaming others for difficulties we create for ourselves.

Think about how important this process is for the children in our homes and the kids in our churches. Although the concept may not be easy for them to grasp, its demonstration will affect them in ways beyond anything we can imagine.

Family Tie 3: Practice the Golden Rule and Follow the Winners

We need to think seriously about reestablishing the Golden Rule in our families. It could make such a redemptive difference. What if we parents tried to become kids again, so we could see how tough it is today for children who face temptations in school? What would happen if we could really understand the peer pressure, the drugs, the pregnancies, the doubt, the fear, the abuse, the guns and the gangs?

Young people need guidance, too, in every stage of life. Think what it means to the girl who goes to a new high school for the first time, to the boy who finds the first hair on his chest or hears his voice change, to newlyweds who come home from their honeymoon to decide who will keep the checkbook. There are a thousand places along the human journey where we need folks to apply the Golden Rule to such relationships with us. And there are just as many places where we need to apply the Golden Rule to our relationships with them.

If each of us in the family practiced the Golden Rule, we would begin to realize how things feel and look to others. Then we could be more accepting and loving at home and would help make home and family sanctuaries where we experience peace, acceptance and strength.

I (H. B.) like to think of 1 Corinthians 13:4-7 (*NKJV*) as the credo for Christian marriage and family life: "Love . . . is kind; . . . thinks no evil; does not rejoice in iniquity, but rejoices in the truth; bears all things, believes all things, hopes all things, endures all things." That is so much different than the all-too-common idea that home is where you are treated the best but grumble the most.

No one can build a satisfying home alone. Each of us has to be brought into the process and must see home as a special place for spiritual refueling and emotional renewal. I enjoy telling people that if they want happy homes, they must follow the winners. That is, we must look for those who are succeeding in family relationships and try to duplicate what they are doing, saying and thinking. If we learn from the champions, we can replicate what works in their primary relationships. The winning families seek first the kingdom of God. Strength and empowerment will flow from our determination to put God first in everything that relates to our family. This Kingdom-first lifestyle is the most satisfying life to be found anywhere.

I remember a family that had a strong influence on our family. In many ways they taught our boys strong, respectful behavior that shows even now in the families our sons have established. Their style of life was contagious. When they were together, we could tell they were proud of one another, and the children respected their father and were deeply proud of their mother. They were attentive and polite to one another. When difficulties came, they moved to support, love and lift. Supportive behavior seemed natural to them. They never raised their voices. As Scripture teaches, they refused to provoke one another to anger, but they kept encouraging one another to be the best that they could be. Follow the example of people like that.

If we are to have a strong marriage, we must practice the Golden Rule and imitate winners.

Family Tie 4: Practice Forgiveness and Build Each Other Up

In Ephesians 4:32 *(NKJV)*, Paul wrote to the church at Ephesus that they were to "be kind to one another, tenderhearted, forgiving one another, even as God in Christ forgave you." What an order, what a gift to another and what a relief to us. Forgiveness is to our relationships what oil is to a machine: We simply cannot operate without it.

Jesus, Paul and serious Christian disciples in every century have taught that forgiveness is an absolute necessity.

Forgiveness is to our relationships what oil is to a machine: We simply cannot operate without it.

One of the greatest deterrents to a satisfying family life is our failing to forgive another family member. We owe it to each other and to ourselves to set a mood in our homes that is open and free and relaxed and forgiving.

The apostle Paul offered good spiritual direction and sound emotional counsel when he said, "Do not let the sun go down while you are still angry" (Eph. 4:26, *NIV*). Closing a day without repairing a misunderstanding means that we will have a troubled night and a troubled tomorrow. It is possible to hold grudges to the point that we make our future ghastly and ourselves miserable. Healthy families know how to forgive and forget.

One way to cultivate forgiveness is for each of us to ask ourselves, *What kind of friend am I?* I (H. B.) raise that question in family counseling. People often respond by saying, "What do you mean, what kind of friends are we? We're married. We're brothers and sisters. We live in the same house. What do you mean, what kind of friends are we?"

I hasten to add, "How do friends treat each other?" Then I remind them, "Friends say 'I'm sorry' when they offend each other. Friends offer compliments when one does something admirable. They say, 'That's okay,' when others have wronged them. Friends, rather than hold a grudge or become angry, value each other. They encourage each other. They challenge each other to be their very best."

If our families are going to be as good as they can be, our family members must become authentic friends. When we disagree with our spouse, we should ask ourselves, *Why are we doing this to each other when we are so important to each other?* Or we should say to them, "We are the most important people in the world to each other. We should be loving and build each other up." Let's be as nice to our spouse and children as we are to our friends.

Family Tie 5: Grow Spiritually and Expect God to Build Your Home

At a trying moment in national life, Joshua announced these strong words of determined resolve: "If it seems evil to you to serve the LORD, choose for yourselves this day whom you will serve . . . But as for me and my house, we will serve the LORD" (Josh. 24:15, *NKJV*).

Our families, churches and nation need thousands of people to make a Joshua-type commitment concerning "me and my house." Regardless of what the Smiths and the Joneses and the Greens do, we have determined our course of action. We can read all the books we want on marriage, family and mentoring of children, but they will do little good without our commitment to make Christ head of our family.

Making Him the head involves a set of our will so that He is first in all things. We make Him the head of the family. We allow Him to evaluate every conversation and decision and priority. He is the invited one because He never forces Himself into our human relationships. He is our pattern, our guide, our ideal.

When such a commitment is in place, we already know what we will do when inevitable conflicts develop and storms appear. God's Son, our Lord Jesus, is the finest source for sound, healthy family relationships. We need to make our commitment to Him so definite that the whole family already knows how we need to respond when trouble stalks our way.

We need to think through our responses to the values of secular society before they entangle us even more than they have. In Romans 12, the apostle Paul wrote that we should not let the world squeeze us into its mold (see v. 2). The forces of the world will determine our values and will establish our standard of morality unless we intentionally resist. We will embrace a self-centered and materialistic value system unless we resist it. We need to build Christian values into family life the way we build good health practices and sound nutritional habits. We must develop a fixed will that puts God first in all things.

Following God's will is never automatic. It must be intentional. But to be intentional, we must start with the belief that God always has our best interests in mind. A sad reality in our world is the failure of many Christians to follow God's will in their family. They miss God's plans for them and experience unrest, unhappiness, failure and fragmented relationships. Years later they experience the awful harvest of family brokenness, pain, divorce and alienation.

Why not avoid all of this by instituting a Joshua-type family commitment: "As for me and my house, we will serve the Lord"? The Joshua mind-set creates a home where God is supreme, where God indwells our hearts to such a degree that He takes up residence.

Then He directs our lives better than we could ever do on our own. He takes charge because we ask Him to do so. He leads our family in better ways than we could ever devise on our own. When we commit our family and ourselves as Joshua did, God leads us to incredibly fulfilling accomplishments and takes us places we never dream of going. His ways are ways of peace, joy, satisfaction and accomplishment.

Once while being entertained as the honored dinner guest with a new family, I (H. B.) noticed they had a chair and table setting for one more person than had arrived. The hostess invited us to come to the table. When everyone gathered, I asked if another guest was expected and suggested we might wait.

"He's already here," they responded. I was puzzled and asked them to explain. "We always set an extra plate for the master. We have a tendency to not be as careful as we should in our speech, so the extra place setting reminds us Jesus is listening to every conversation. We want to be sure we are as much like Him as possible. We want Jesus to know He is welcome. We want Him to dominate our lifestyle and our conversation and our values. Making a place for Him makes all the difference for us. Although some people may think it strange, it reminds us that we belong to Him. You might call it a holy show-and-tell."

Although we might not set a place at the table for Jesus, we can live a life of continual dependence on Him and welcome Him into every facet of our family life.

MARRIAGE HAS A LOT TO DO
WITH THE CHURCH

"Why talk about marriage and family?" a family specialist asked. He then answered his own question, "Because our own family experience is the most significant experience of our lives. As a human interaction, it has greater impact on our lives than any other experience." Thus, the Christian faith, designed by God to invade every nook and cranny of life, has many ways to strengthen marriages. Marriage, faith, parenting and holy enablement are all connected.

The driving force behind the writing of this book is our belief that the Church must do everything it can to develop spiritually strong and emotionally healthy kids. To accomplish this goal, the family of God must do all it can to build strong marriages and to develop healthy families.

Because a desire for a strong Christ-centered marriage is more caught than taught, our churches must work to become laboratories of healthy family relationships. Our goal should be to make every Christian marriage a training camp for the children from that marriage and to provide a model for every child who observes from outside the family.

While developing satisfying marriages may not be our church's only priority, we must consider one marriage-ministry specialist's assessment: "The heart of family ministry is the nature of the church, not merely its work."[15]

Serving people and helping them establish relationships at home are the heart of a church's work. The research and literature inside and outside the Christian community supports the premise that America's problems with children are really problems with adults. And those adult problems often relate to marriage and family.

WILL YOUR FAMILY SURVIVE AND THRIVE?

If the Christian family in America survives, it will be because we pay whatever price it takes to turn our families back to God and His plans for us. We believe God will see to it that the Christian family survives in an ultimate sense, but the more pressing question for us is, Will our family survive? Will it be authentically Christian? Will it be a source of grace and love and forgiveness? Will it be an enjoyable experience? Will it be a family that children from broken homes can follow as a model for their own future families? The Lord Jesus wants us to have such a spiritually strong family.

We pray for children
who tease little sisters and wonder why they tattle,
who giggle and say precocious things and love life,
who play Peekaboo with grandfatherly types in restaurants;

and we pray for children
who have absentee fathers who never call,
whose lives have no connection to what they see on TV
who live with the reality of children crippled and killed by war
and terrorists.

CHAPTER 11

THIRTY-NINE WAYS TO IMPROVE OUR IMPACT ON KIDS

We Can Make a Difference

More than 70 million children, many of whom are at spiritual and economic risk, need what God intends a church to offer. But how do we—ordinary people in ordinary churches with ordinary energy and ordinary imaginations—meet that need?

Our preaching and teaching about God's plan for the human family and the family of God—His Church—serve as the foundation. That means we stress the spiritual development of the biological family. That means we become family to those who have no family. That means every congregation must be continually reminded of the disastrous consequences our society and individuals can expect from anything less than a Christ-centered church and healthy family relationships.

It's time to counteract the harm that society, the media and so-called political correctness do to undermine family values and to destroy innocent kids. With every ounce of holy energy that God provides, we must fight the increasingly pervasive notion that alternative family lifestyles are acceptable replacements for the way God intends us to live.

Our communication must be so clear that people who consider seeking a divorce will know that they are setting themselves up for lifelong problems and pain.

Our communication must be so clear that teens know the consequences of premarital sex, including pregnancy, disease, a heavy conscience, death and undermining the sexual adjustments of their eventual marriage.

Our communication must be so efficient that members of the Church know how vital righteousness is in their parenting. This communication must be so efficient that everyone in the Church has an accurate assessment of what is happening to our children.

STRATEGIES TO CORRECT A COMMON FALLACY

Before we discuss specific strategies to accomplish effective family-focused ministries, let's consider how to correct a common fallacy. Millions of dollars are invested every year in conferences where pastors attend a seminar or forum presented by some highly visible Christian leader to discover a new method or discuss a problem. Let's acknowledge that trading insights, sharing approaches and discussing principles are useful and helpful—often even stimulating. But a ministry that thrives in one place may not work in another.

Thousands of churches could increase their productivity in a month or less if the pastor and lay leaders would practice what highly effective leaders have done in other settings: Start with a problem or need; research it thoroughly; count resources of finance, facility and personnel; and then get the most spiritually alert people in their church to unite in prayer to find a way to meet the recognized need. In a little while, God will inspire the creative imagination of someone in the congregation with a plan that uniquely fits the situation. Then as the plan is implemented with God's blessing, people will be won and helped.

Perhaps this process seems too simple or impractical. It is not intended to be without work and travail. Rather, it is a way to use a combination of commitments and ownership of those people who care most about our churches. It involves a holy wait before God with brothers and sisters of the faith. It is the people of God seeking guidance for the work of God among people who need God most.

We should check out the witnesses to this approach and read what they wrote and listen to what they say. Soon we will discover this was the approach taken by Rick Warren, Mother Teresa, Bill Bright, Bill Hybels and Henrietta Mears.

Each of them saw a need, sought all the information and data they could discover, studied Scripture, prayed with spiritually mature people and then applied all the creative imagination he or she could to the effort. Then these godly leaders developed a customized plan that worked for them through their ministry in a specific setting at a particular time.

We must dare to believe God has a unique plan for every church.

We must dare to believe God has a unique plan for every church. Let us open our hearts to hear what God wants by praying with John Baillie:

> *O holy Spirit of God, visit now this soul of mine . . .*
> *Inspire all my thoughts.*
> *Pervade my imagination.*
> *Suggest all my decisions.*
> *Be with me in my speech and my silence.[1]*

THIRTY-NINE WAYS TO FOCUS OUR CHURCHES ON KIDS' NEEDS

1. Use God's values to counter secular values.

This can be done in our preaching, teaching and living. Let's tell it well. The Christian lifestyle is the most fulfilling way to live that anyone has ever discovered. We need to speak up about the Ten Commandments. Pastors can underscore the distinctions between scriptural and secular views of marriage, family and child rearing as they conduct marriage ceremonies, do pastoral counseling and informally interact with members of the congregation.

2. Model healthy Christian families.

We need to invest time, effort and money in making our family an example of what a spiritually and emotionally healthy family can be. Although the modeling is desirable and convincing to others, the real payoff is the joy and satisfaction we receive from doing it. This effort is not just for families with young children at home. It can be modeled in grown families, empty nesters and golden agers, too.

3. Build our churches into a support system.

When kids are threatened or abused, when marriages are stressed, when teenagers rebel, our churches can become a support system for hurting people. And in the process, it becomes a place where fractured lives can be reassembled after the storm subsides.

4. Organize a mentoring system for children.

Here's an incredibly powerful way one contemporary church builds extended family relationships in its fellowship. Miles McPherson and Wayne Rice tell about a multiracial, inner-city congregation with a burden for reaching teens who have few positive adult role models in their lives. The youth leaders recruit adult church members as mentors to teach young people life skills. Another group of mentors in the same church periodically take teens to work, so youths can see how responsible Christians earn a living. And another group of adults adopts teens as prayer partners.[2] Responsible, Christ-motivated adults will grow spiritually strong as a result of this mentoring relationship, even as the teens grow. The congregation's vision is that someone out of this group of teens will make a startling difference in urban problems in the next generation.

5. Look to Scripture for answers.

In all areas of ministry, we must take the teachings about children and family life from Scripture and make sure everyone in our churches understands them and also knows how to apply them to family relationships.

6. Implement divorce care corps.

We need to organize small groups whose main ministry is to stay close to people in our churches who are going through a divorce. This is a time when people drop out of church when caring is most needed. The divorce is a loss experience where one's grieving resembles the death of a mate or child. Our churches should offer small care groups who make frequent contact, helping them find ways to become more deeply involved in a church and helping the church realize that divorce often is the last thing the divorcee really wanted.

7. Aid broken families, especially the children.

We must support adults and children from broken families so they can rebuild their lives in an environment of love and understanding rather than in an environment of isolation and alienation.

8. Cherish kids on all levels of church life.

When we serve children, we have their futures in our hearts and our hands. There is something wonderful about being able to shape lives that will have an influence long after we are gone. Our present situation is desperate. We're talking life and death. We're talking about kids being disabled emotionally and spiritually for life. We're talking about children never knowing a stable family life. We're talking about kids who have no idea of the value of human life. We're talking about a world where gunfire is the second leading cause of death among Americans ages 10 to 19, where a child is killed every 92 minutes by gunfire.[3]

9. Insist on family purity among lay and clergy leaders.

Some churches, with a notion of tolerance, have allowed leaders to be less pure than the general population. God will not stomach such sinfulness. A sexually mixed-up young adult told one of us in a counseling situation, "One of the reasons I am so messed up is because of the *Peyton Place* stuff I saw in the church where I grew up. Nearly everyone had a sexual hang-up, and we all knew about it." This cannot be allowed in our churches. God expects church leaders to be pure and chaste, and He enables them to live such a life.

10. Carry placards and write letters.

We have a responsibility to lead our churches to influence political leaders who draft and vote on community, state and national policy. We must be firm, sensible and Christian, and we must present children who have few lobbyists to speak for them.

11. Train ourselves to view children by their potential.

It's easy to see how present negative trends in our society will produce negative results in children. On the contrary, we can predict positive spiritual results with children. The 12- and 13-

year-olds in our present youth groups will be heads of families in 15 to 20 years. What kinds of families will they head?

12. Align the family of God and the human family.

They are our two last bastions for meaning and righteousness. Pastor Richard Dobbins said it well: "The natural family was designed by God to procreate, nurture, strengthen and sustain life from birth to death. In much the same way, the church, as the spiritual family of God, has been designed to evangelize, nurture, discipline, strengthen, and sustain the life of God's children."[4] Our church members must try to see family issues as being directly related to the mission of our churches.

Years ago, in an article in *Religion in Life*, Samuel L. Hamilton wrote, "The church cannot function as she should in a disordered world unless she employs the home as her main reliance in Christian nurture."[5] That's still true for us today.

13. Resource the home.

We must continually avoid the temptation of expecting a church to provide all of the Christian training children receive. Because of the relatively small amount of time children spend at church, comprehensive training cannot be accomplished even if they are involved in everything a church provides, including Sunday School, Vacation Bible School, weekend club/Bible study and children's church. The discouraging dilemma is that many parents do not know how to give their kids Christian training. They will never learn how to do it without purposeful attempts by their local church to teach them.

14. Maintain strong outreach contacts with unchurched families.

Ministering to children without trying to spiritually impact their families is like placing adhesive bandages on the wounds caused by a traumatic car accident. Parents often are more open to a church's outreach efforts than we think. We have a church planter friend who has organized a new church called the Family Church—"where you'll feel right at home." A mass mailer from his church communicated this idea in a headline that read, "At first we went for our children; now we go to church for all of us." The advertising copy continued: "Perhaps you are like a lot of concerned parents—looking for a place for your family to develop spiritually and learn more about God. If you've given up on church or consider yourself a 'non-churchgoer,' you'll be in good company. Over 70 percent of our congregation describe themselves that way. At least they did before they started attending the Family Church. Come and check out this young and growing congregation some Sunday morning at 10:00—you owe it to yourself and your family."

We need to think of all the parents of children who come to church alone as people who need our churches. Every church should focus on reaching out to those families in every possible way. They have already trusted us with their most prized possessions.

15. Avoid overscheduling.
Age-appropriate activities at our churches nurture children, but we must balance them against the need for family time. Some of our churches do not schedule church activities at least one or two nights each week, and we should encourage church families to use those evenings as times to spend together and to nurture the family.

16. Provide family-together activities.
More and more families, especially those that live a great distance from their extended families, need church activities that include two or more generations. Examples might include all-

church fellowship activities where families eat together, church services where family members attend and sit together, musical programs where people from all generations are asked to participate, and cross-generational craft activities. Some churches conduct family outreach activities so that kids and early teens are part of the ministry. Another church has two or three families together call on older people who cannot leave their homes as well as residents of nursing facilities.

17. Establish parenting support groups.

The idea is to network parents with other parents who are facing the same issues in child rearing. Information is made available and parenting skills are sharpened during these sessions. People also are encouraged to share their experiences and to express their love and support for one another. The following are some suggested topics:

- Caring for newborns
- Dealing with TV's impact on kids
- Matching family devotions to a child's development
- Coping with the strong-willed kids
- Applying the Bible to the child's life
- Modeling faith at home

18. Inform parents about what is being taught at church.

Our Sunday School teachers can do this by periodically sending notes to each home and explaining lessons that are being studied; by placing notices in the bulletin and newsletter about what is being covered in Sunday School; by encouraging parents to visit their children's Sunday School class; and by having a special reception for parents and children like a parent-teacher conference in the public schools.

19. Provide support to parents of rebellious children.

Often a child's rebellion has to be borne alone by parents, who suffer grief about their loss of relationship. They feel like failures. Many different voices tell them to do such things as "Put them out," "Let them do what they want." It's a difficult choice and most parents have little experience or help in dealing with such problems.

20. Upgrade the children's Christian education programs.

In the technological revolution that is taking place in education, children sometimes have state-of-the-art educational experiences at school and horse-and-buggy experiences at our churches. Although our churches may not have all the latest tools available, we should provide the best possible children's Christian education program.

21. Build relationships with kids in the community.

We should consider these approaches for starters: preschool, mother's day out, day care, tutorial programs, after-school study hall at church, English as a second language classes, soccer camp, basketball camp and day camp. An inner-city church, for example, could install basketball hoops in its parking lot and permit neighborhood kids to play there.

**22. Implement annual prayer summits
to pray for children.**

We can schedule this once each year on a Sunday evening, a weekday evening or a Saturday morning. The summit should probably be no more than three hours in length. Everyone who attends should be given a list of children's names for whom to pray. At some time during the summit, conditions in which the children live should be discussed. Teachers who serve in the public schools should be prayed for.

Before the summit closes, the group should pray especially for divine guidance about what the Lord wants them to do for kids. We may want to include in the prayer concerns that children may fear the Lord and serve Him (see Deut. 6:13), know God personally early in life (see 2 Chron. 34:1-3), hate evil (see Ps. 97:10), have a responsible attitude in all personal relationships (see Rom. 13:8), desire the right kind of friends (see Prov. 1:10,15) and trust the Lord for direction in their lives (see Prov. 3:5-6).

23. Provide mandatory and effective premarital counseling.
This is part of the prevention and preservation effort for good marriages and is a background for rearing strong Christian children. Some time ago, Jeannette and Robert Lauer conducted a study called Marriages Made to Last. They interviewed 300 couples who had been married for 15 years or longer. They asked couples to select from 39 statements those that best illustrated why their marriages have lasted. The following are some of the most often chosen responses:

- My spouse is my best friend.
- I like my spouse as a person.
- Marriage is a long-term commitment.
- Marriage is sacred.
- We agree on aims and goals.
- My spouse has grown more interesting.
- I want the relationship to succeed.
- An enduring marriage is important to social stability.
- We laugh together.[6]

24. Give priority to single parents.
We must make ministry to single parents inclusive and visible. Single parents have to accomplish nearly everything alone,

including earning a living, maintaining the house, participating at school and church and transporting children to various activities. Specialized ministries and support groups help. However, frequently what single parents need most is the opportunity to be included in the life of a church. That means they must be welcomed and provided with child care and transportation, if necessary.

25. Check out the Responsible Fatherhood program.

The United States Department of Health and Human Services has a program called Responsible Fatherhood. This two-pronged program supports competitive grants to faith-based and community organizations that strengthen fathers' involvement in the lives of children and supports grants to mentor children of prisoners. This growing mission field is made up of nearly 25 million children who seldom, if ever, see their fathers.

26. Develop small groups.

Two of the most popular types are support groups and growth groups. Every bookstore has material on how to organize small groups. To use Charles Swindoll's words, small groups are "the part that touches people by bringing the gospel up close."[7] George Whitefield, the great statesman of Methodism, said, "None that truly loves his own soul and his brethren as himself will be shy of opening his heart in order to have their advice, reproof, admonition and prayer, as occasion requires. A sincere person will esteem it one of the greatest blessings."[8]

27. Experiment with intergenerational ministries.

The purpose is to allow children to become friends with adults and adults to become friends with kids. A good way for us to start is to plan a program similar to the learning components that might take place in a third- or fourth-grade Sunday School class: storytelling, crafts and songs, maybe some action choruses. We then separate the group into smaller groups of five or six people that include people from three generations who are also unrelated to each other. For example, in one church, each group studied the biblical story about Joseph's coat of many colors, and then each group made a coat out of paper gowns like those used in physicians' offices.

Another church had a program in which younger teens were responsible for attending the senior citizens' Christmas party, and each teen was to make friends with one golden ager. Before the meeting was over, they sang duets and solos and trios of Christmas carols, and people from both age groups talked about their time together. Family church camping is another opportunity for intergenerational impact.

28. Arrange adopt-a-kid family camping.

An intact Christian family could adopt a child from an unchurched home for the camp. Or a church might form weekend extended family groups with single people in the church and kids whose families do not attend church. If these children then attend church, they will know someone there.

29. Provide sex education at church.

At times, people in our churches have criticized public schools for offering sex education. The arguments maintain public schools do not teach Christian values about sexuality, family and parenting. The objections also say this education should be left to the home and the church. After these arguments are made and accepted, it is imperative for the home and those of us in the local church to move into this area to teach values. Some parents will need help, and our churches should be prepared to offer that training.

30. Offer parenting classes.

Although most of us would not admit it, we know very little about parenting. We will learn with practice, but sometimes that knowledge comes too late to correct mistakes. The church should arrange for an expert to speak or ask three mature couples to tell about their successes and failures. Most of the problems we parents face would be easier to bear if we realized that other people have faced the same difficulties and have found answers.

Most of the problems we parents face would be easier to bear if we realized that other people have faced the same difficulties and have found answers.

31. Absorb singles into the family of God.

When we talk with singles, it soon becomes apparent that one of their biggest problems is feeling left out at church. Opening our churches to singles means including them in elections, social activities, committees and teaching. Many churches would do a great service to kids if singles were involved in children's ministries, something like a big brother or big sister program. Family specialist Charles Sell said, "When the church is like a family, singles can find the family that they need. They not only want involvement; they want close involvement."[9] Singles provide a magnificent source of workers who have the ability to deepen a church's ministry to children.

32. Customize ministry to a particular child.

When Barbara became a widow with two boys, ages 7 and 9, members of the men's fellowship in her small church decided they would help her rear the boys. From the men's group of only 10 members, someone volunteered to do some activity with the boys every month. Within a few months, the boys felt close to most of the men in their church. After two or three years, Barbara married again and moved away, but today her sons, now grown men, are acting as mentors for boys in the churches they attend.

33. Emphasize rituals.

Weddings, baptisms, Communion services and receptions for new church members are all big events in the lives of participants. Our churches need to make a big deal of the rituals, especially those that involve children.

One church invites kids ages 8 and older to help pack Thanksgiving baskets for those with little income or who cannot leave their homes. Another church has a Thanksgiving morning country breakfast—one adult does the cooking and the teens do the serving. They even let the kids elect the layperson of the year and award a trophy to that person at the breakfast.

34. Institute or revitalize the children's sermon.

A while ago, I (Neil) visited a famous old church in San Francisco where the worship style was so wild and the theology so liberal, I hardly knew I was in church. But when the time came for the pastor's sermon for children, he sat on the front of the platform and told the kids about the love of God. I watched the children's eyes, and I could see that they adored their pastor. I also noticed that every adult in the congregation was carefully listening to the sermon intended for kids. Interest level was stronger for the children's sermon than for anything else in that service.

Church will mean something important to those children for the rest of their lives because of how close they felt to their pastor. When we adults are asked about our warmest memories from childhood, we often describe a caring person who touched our lives at a special moment. Why not make that moment the sermon to children?

35. Make the church kid-friendly.

If we were three feet tall and walked into our churches, what would the church facilities say to us? What would our Sunday School room say to us? What impressions would we receive from people who greet us at the door? One pastor we know whose church has an attendance of about 400 knows every child by name. He has dedicated many of them to Christ, and he plans to be their pastor when they are old enough to be elected to official decision-making groups. Another pastor joked, "Being nice to children is my job security for the future."

36. Provide family-life skills training.

Charles Sell provides a list of concerns that members of one congregation gave when asked what areas of training were of most interest to them. Out of 45 choices, here are the most popular responses: marriage enrichment, marriage communication, family communication, roles of husband and wife, teaching Christian values at home, parenting young children, marital conflict resolution, leading children to Christ, marital problem solving, finances and money management, and family worship—family spiritual time.[10]

The list might differ between churches, but that list indicated that people in our churches wanted help with marriage issues, family issues and spiritual development. One church determined to plan one family training event about every three months, including marriage-enrichment weekends, how to get along with parents for teens, dads discipling dads and marriage-maintenance seminars.

37. Emphasize teen abstinence.

Because we as Christians know there are significant benefits resulting from sexual purity and sexual abstinence before marriage, a program like the Southern Baptist conference called True Love Waits should be considered by every one of our churches. Give this research some thought: "Calling it 'the most poignant finding of their study,' researchers writing in the *Journal of Youth and Adolescence* reported that 43 percent of sexually experienced teens wish they hadn't engaged in premarital intercourse."[11]

38. Hold a "What Is Needed?" forum.

Now that we are more aware of the problems facing children and families, we should invite a group of 10 or 12 people to a brainstorming session where we talk about the needs of kids in our church. Make a list of

What does God want us to do?

the needs and then think creatively in the group about how those needs might be met with our existing facilities and personnel. Perhaps a mission-search group could grow out of this meeting—a group of people committed to meet for prayer and Bible study once each week with the express purpose of determining how our church or our group could better serve children. Some churches have discovered great benefits from such a group whose Bible study and prayer meetings focus on the question, What does God want us to do? Such prayer often provides a clear focus of the need, the available resources and helpful motivation for getting started.

39. Put on "potential" glasses.

I (Neil) will need a paragraph or two to explain this suggestion. As I write the last pages of this book, I have a tear in my eye as I think of the alarming issues we have faced together as writer and reader. With all my heart I pray that we all have a new commitment and a new love for serving children. What a journey of discovery it has been trying to think through and share these ideas.

I want to tell a story I read in a book called *Creating Community*. I purchased the book because I wanted to hear what people outside the Church thought community was and what it should accomplish. When I read the book, I discovered it was saturated with ideas about how lonely people seek community and how a sense of community can be built. I don't recall, however, that in 330 pages it ever mentioned the Church. I kept thinking as I read, *Community is the Church's business. The Church has been in the fellowship and caring business for 2,000 years.*

Let me share still more about my frustration and about my hope.

The book tells a powerful story about a sophisticated urban unmarried secularist who, at 42, found herself eight months pregnant with her first child and deserted by the father, who told her he had no plans to continue living with her or to support the child. Feeling alone and terrified, the woman didn't know what to do.

When we met her in the book, she was surrounded by about two dozen women, men and children who were throwing her a baby shower. The gifts were the usual fare for baby showers but included something unusual: The guests promised to be with her during delivery, to help her bring the baby home from the hospital, to support her emotionally, to help with babysitting and to stay in her life as much as possible until the baby was grown.

Then they assured her that they counted it a priceless treasure to be able to have a part in her baby's life. Her patched-together family of friends gave her one loud and clear message: We'll be here for you.

I wondered if the Church would do a thing like that. I'm hopeful the Church will someday, maybe soon, welcome every kid with that kind of enthusiasm. Of course, we can't approve of the sins of the parents, but as Jesus said, when we receive a child, it is as if we receive Him (see Matt. 18:5; Mark 9:37; Luke 9:48).

The above list of ways to serve children is only a beginning. The specific steps of improved ministry to children are not nearly as important as our caring and loving. The most vital ministries to children generally start by people praying, "Oh, Lord, what can we do?" We need to start praying that prayer now, and God will impress us with challenging and rewarding ways to help save our kids.

THE CHURCH FOR THE NEW GENERATION

This book has been dedicated to our grandchildren and to all of the kids everywhere who will carry the mantle of Jesus Christ in this new millennium. In their behalf we offer these final words concerning the Church we covet for them.

Taylor, Amanda, Hilary, Jeffrey, William and Katie are the next generation of the Londons and Wisemans, and they are very important to us. We are sure that you could add the names of precious children in your life as well. Know that we are concerned about them, too.

When we think about kids and their future in our world, it's easy to forget the admonition of Scripture, "Do not be anxious about anything" (Phil. 4:6, *NIV*).

One of the great Church leaders in the United States was asked how the future of the Church looked to him. He turned to his inquirer and spelled out Y-O-U-T-H. He's right. The only hope for our world is for the Church of Jesus Christ to build up children in the nurture and admonition of the Lord, and for the Church to invest its efforts in children everywhere, inside and outside the Church.

May I (H. B.) put my concerns for the next generation in the first-person?

When I was a young father and pastor, I took for granted that my children would be reared in a church family that would fill in the gaps my wife, Bev, and I missed. Brad and Bryan, from their births, were loved by the congregations we served. They had wonderful role models in youth leaders and other families in our churches. And we are grateful. Neil and his wife, Bonnie, feel the same about the way the churches they were privileged to lead loved their sons, Todd and Scott.

As I look back on those churches, especially during our sons' formative years, I am reminded that they had activities that were positive and leaders who made them know they had worth and value. Today, they are wonderful Christian husbands and fathers largely because of the influences of those churches on their lives. Were our children perfect? No way. They made as many mistakes as other kids make, but the churches loved them just the same. I know Bev and I made a lot of mistakes in rearing our boys that we would remedy if we had the opportunity. Yet, as we look back over the journey, we thank God for the family of God that helped us raise and influence our family.

Twelve Things I Covet

What about the next generation? What should a church be, and how should a church set its priorities? Although the following thoughts are not scholarly nor are they novel, they are things I covet for members of the new generation who will populate our churches in the years to come.

1. A church that is led by a faithful pastor

I want children to have a minister who is consistent and effective in his or her own family living and has a shepherd-servant spirit for everyone in the congregation. I want kids to have a pastor who knows them by name, who cares about them, who takes time to listen to them. I want them to have a pastor whose messages are relevant and geared to real-life issues. I want children to have a pastor who loves them as Jesus loved the children He met along the way.

2. A church that is biblically based

I want a church for them that preaches and practices the essential truths of the Word of God, a church where the Word of God determines the work of the church.

I want a church for them that will insist on the basic principles of morality as taught by Jesus in the Sermon on the Mount and one that takes seriously the admonition to live by the Ten Commandments. I want kids to be encouraged to memorize and to apply the Word of God to their lives.

3. A church that is financially generous

I want all children to have a church home where budgeting for the educational ministries for children and young people has high priority. I covet that leaders will understand that to effectively teach and reach kids and young people, they may have to make a much larger investment than they make in other ministries. Such an investment will pay off because members of the next generation will know they are loved, cared for and valued by their church.

4. A church that trains parents

Today, parenting may be the most difficult assignment in the world. I realize we can't force-feed parents, but I also realize that every church needs a mentoring program whereby younger couples can identify with older, more established Christian families. This follows the teaching of 2 Timothy 2:2, which commands faithful men to teach what they have learned to the next generation.

5. A church that is served by dedicated laypeople

I know churches often need paid professionals as they grow larger. In reality, only 3 in 10 churches have more than 1 paid professional. But I want children to be influenced and loved by laypeople. Some of my most memorable moments in a church were those times when a lay leader loved me in spite of my faults and fears. They were wonderful people who loved God and felt called to walk alongside a young person. Granted, lay leaders need training, and the Church needs to remember that the greatest fear anyone has when given ministry opportunities is the fear of not knowing how.

6. A church that teaches respect for authority

Authority that is based on scriptural principles—respect for the authority of parents, church, government and the educational system—is essential. Every young person needs to respect those people to whom God has given direction to lead in the nation and the Church. I want members of the next generation to know there are people to whom God has given responsibility to watch over them and to give guidance to their lives.

7. A church that knows it is never right nor wise to rebel against God

I want someone to point out the danger of transgression. I want members of the next generation to be confronted about their sins and be given the opportunity to confess, to repent and to be forgiven. I want the truth of the gospel presented to them at an early age so that they can forsake their sins and can develop the Christian lifestyle that God desires for them.

8. A church that teaches servanthood

We live in a complicated, me-oriented society, and if a church does not provide its people opportunities to be "foot washers," it will rob them of a blessing. I hope every church will provide ways for members of the next generation to work in the inner city, to take missionary work trips, to assist older citizens and to care for and help one another when difficulties arise. I want them to experience what it means to come alongside another young person who is experiencing loneliness and failure. I want my grandchildren to have a church that will help them develop a heart like our Lord's.

9. A church that trains children and youths to recognize other Christians

I sincerely want them to learn that many genuine Christians do not see every detail of religious practice or belief in the same way. I hope my grandchildren will never feel superior to other people nor believe they hold the only answers. I covet a church that will preach the truth, protect the absolute and help the next generation make good spiritual choices but never with an attitude of self-righteous superiority.

10. A church that emphasizes a balanced lifestyle

I want dedicated leaders to teach early that stewardship of time, talent and treasure is as important as worship and attendance at church. I pray they are taught the value of tithing, giving of time in service to the Body of Christ and faithfully attending the services of worship.

11. A church that stresses family values

I realize that every home cannot have a mom and dad and biological children. Yet the traditional family can be the benchmark. Our civilization cannot survive without stable homes. In this day, when chastity and morality and fidelity are being denigrated, I covet a church for the next generation that will raise the standard of moral values from its pulpit and in its Sunday School classes.

12. A church that helps people find the real reason for living
The church my grandchildren attend must have a clearly defined mission for its existence. Too many churches apparently exist to support their own survival. I pray for the leaders of the Church for the next generation to possess a worldview that truly believes their community desperately needs Christ. I hope leaders will force their whole congregation to examine its role in society. Beyond that I wish for them a church that will be as interested in the spiritual health of the Church as it is in the number of members who attend and that they will be involved in bringing Christ to their community. I pray the church they attend will enable them to live out the wonderful message of Romans 12:11 (*NKJV*), "Not lagging in diligence, fervent in spirit, serving the Lord."

THE CHURCH I DREAM ABOUT

The Church I dream about for the next generation should be a people of love and of enthusiasm for the gospel, but always vigilant. Like Nehemiah, they will stay alert to anything that might create disillusionment and apathy in the lives of the members of the congregation.

For the next generation, I envision a fellowship of saints who put on the whole armor of God so that when Satan attacks, they can stand firm. If the Lord tarries, I want my grandchildren to come to old age and to look back on their parents, their children and their grandchildren and be able to say about the Church— the authentic family of God—that it is the greatest institution in the world and that they are proud to be a part of it.

That is the Church I covet for the future generations of my family and for yours as well. My reasons for wanting such a Church are explained in this poem penned by an anonymous author:

A builder builded a temple
He wrought with care and skill,
Pillars and spires and arches
Were fashioned to meet his will.
And men said when they saw its beauty,
"It shall never know decay.

Great is thy skill, O Builder,
Thy fame shall endure for aye."

A teacher builded a temple
She wrought with skill and care,
Forming each pillar with patience,
Laying each stone with prayer.
None saw the unceasing effort;
None knew of the marvelous plan
For the temple the teacher builded
Was unseen by the eyes of man.

Gone is the builder's temple
Crumbled into the dust.
Pillar and spires and arches
Food for consuming rust,
But the temple the teacher builded
Shall endure while the ages roll,
For that beautiful unseen temple
Was a child's immortal soul.

ENDNOTES

Introduction

1. The National Institute of Health, "Proceedings from the Conference on *Counting Couples: Improving Marriage, Divorce, Remarriage and Cohabitation Data in the Federal Statistical System*," Childstats.gov. http://www.child stats.gov/ countingcouples (accessed August 25, 2003).

2. U.S. Bureau of the Census, "America's Families and Living Arrangements," *Current Population Reports,* March 2000. http://www.census.gov/ (accessed August 25, 2003), quoted in "What Does a Family Look Like Today?" *Holiness Today* (March 2003), p. 30.

3. U.S. Bureau of the Census, "Profile of Selected Social Characteristics," *American FactFinder,* 2000. http://www.factfinder.census.gov/ (accessed August 25, 2003).

4. Harold Ivan Smith, "Singles: The Family of One," *Holiness Today* (March 2003), p. 31.

5. U.S. Bureau of the Census, "America's Families and Living Arrangements."

6. Ibid.

7. Dennis Rainey, *Ministering to Twenty-First Century Families* (Nashville, TN: Word Publishing, 2001), quoted in "The Un-blended Family," *Leadership* (spring 2002), p. 35.

8. U.S. Bureau of the Census, "America's Families and Living Arrangements."

9. U.S. Department of Health and Human Services, "Promoting Responsible Fatherhood," *U.S. Department of Health and Human Services,* April 26, 2002. http://fatherhood.hhs.gov (accessed August 25, 2003).

10. Barbara Schiller, "Single Parent Sunday," *Leadership* (spring 2002), p. 47.

11. U.S. Bureau of the Census, "Nearly 5.5 Children Live with Grandparents, Census Bureau Reports," July 1, 1999. http://www.census.gov/Press-Release/www/1999/cb99-115.html (accessed August 28, 2003).

12. Ibid.

13. *USA Today,* January 29, 2002, quoted in "States of the Union," *Leadership* (spring 2002), p. 13.

14. Les and Leslie Parrott, "Today's Family: Holding Tough in Tough Times," *Holiness Today* (March 2003), p. 15.

15. U.S. Divorce Statistics, "Index of Divorce Statistics," *Divorce Magazine.* http://www.divorcemagazine.com/survey/ (accessed August 25, 2003).

16. Les and Leslie Parrott, "Today's Family: Holding Tough in Tough Times," p. 15.

17. U.S. Bureau of the Census, "America's Families and Living Arrangements."

18. Ibid.

19. Chris Stinnett, "They Live Together and Attend Your Church," *Leadership* (spring 2002), p. 49.

20. Adrienne Washington, "PG Deaths Refocus Spotlight on Domestic Violence," *The Washington Times,* March 18, 2003, n.p.

21. Ibid.

22. Ibid.

23. Ibid.

24. Barna Research Group, "Born Again Christians," *Barna Research Online.* http://www.barna.org/cgi-bin/home.asp (accessed August 23, 2003).

25. Ibid.

26. "News in Religion," *Holiness Today* (March 2003), p. 41, quoted at *Crosswalk.com.* http://www.crosswalk.com/news/religiontoday/ (accessed n.d.)

27. Barna Research Group, "This Year's Intriguing Findings," *Barna Research Online,* December 17, 2001. http://www.barna.org/cgi-bin/home.asp (accessed August 28, 2003).

28. Barna Research Group, "Adults Who Attend Church as Children Show Lifelong Effects," *Barna Research Online,* November 5, 2001. http://www.barna.org/cgi-bin/home.asp (accessed August 28, 2003).

29. Barna Research Group, "Is America's Faith Really Shifting?" *Barna Research Online,* February 24, 2003. http://www.barna.org/cgi-bin/home.asp (accessed August 28, 2003).

30. Barna Research Group, *Barna Research Online,* September 17, 2002. http://www.barna.org/cgi-bin/home.asp (accessed August 28, 2003).

31. Edward Hindson, "Changing the Course of a Nation Through Prayer," *National Liberty Journal* (September 26, 2002), n.p.

32. "Revival Report," October 1999, p. 2, quoted in *Current Thoughts and Trends* (January 2000), p. 18.

Chapter 1

1. Dan Kindlon, *Tough Times, Strong Children* (New York: Hyperion Press, 2002), p. vii.

2. "A Time Line of Recent Worldwide School Shootings," *Information Please,* March 23, 2003. http://www.infoplease.com/ipa/A0777958.html (accessed August 23, 2003).

3. Sam Nunn, "Intellectual Honesty, Moral and Ethical Behavior" (speech presented at the National Prayer Breakfast, Washington, D.C., February 1, 1996), printed in *Vital Speeches of the Day* (March 15, 1996), p. 328.

4. Source unknown.

5. Chris Billman, "Try Listening to Your Kids," *Denver Post*, April 25, 1999, sec. H, p. 1.

6. William Pollack, *Real Boys* (New York: Henry Holt and Company, 1998), p. xix.

7. Elizabeth Austin, "A Small Plea to Delete a Ubiquitous Expletive," *U.S. News and World Report* (April 6, 1998), pp. 58-59.

8. Stephen L. Carter, "We Interrupt This Childhood," *Christianity Today* (July 9, 2001), p. 53.

9. Kathleen Parker, "Narcissism Linked to Shootings," *Denver Post*, April 28, 1999, sec. B, p. 11.

10. Kindlon, *Tough Times, Strong Children*, p. 12.

11. Saint Teresa of Avila, *Interior Castle* (New York: Doubleday Image Books, 1961), p. 38.

12. Os Guiness, *The American Hour* (New York: Freedom Press, 1993), p. 310.

13. Darrell Scott, (speech presented to the United States House of Representatives Subcommittee on Crime, House Judiciary Committee, Washington, D.C., May 27, 1999).

14. Ibid.

15. Ibid.

16. Ken Hamblin, "Putting God Back in Our Lives," *Denver Post*, April 25, 1999, sec. H, p. 2.

Chapter 2

1. Elizabeth Akers Allen, "Rock Me to Sleep," quoted in *Bartlett's Familiar Quotations* (Boston: Little, Brown and Company, 1980), p. 610.

2. Os Guiness, *The American Hour* (New York: Freedom Press, 1993), p. 309.

3. "Did You Know . . . ?" *Fifty Ways to Save Our Children*, http://www.50ways.org/ (accessed August 25, 2003).

4. Compassion International, "How to Make a Child a Hero" promotional folder, n.p.

5. Bob Herbert, "Young, Jobless, Hopeless," *The New York Times*, February 6, 2003, sec. A, p. 39.

6. Marie Winn, *Children Without Childhood* (New York: Pantheon Books, 1983), p. 207.

7. Vance Packard, *Our Endangered Children: Growing Up in a Changing World* (Boston: Little, Brown and Company, 1983), p. 26.

8. U.S. Bureau of the Census, *America's Children at Risk* (Washington, D.C.: Government Printing Office, 1997), n.p.

9. Elizabeth Kolbert, "Whose Family Values Are They, Anyway?" *The New York Times*, August 6, 1995.

10. Barbara Dafoe Whitehead, "The Divorce Culture," *Atlantic Monthly* (1993), quoted in Beverly Cleary, *The Children's Story of Divorce* (New York: Alfred A. Knopf, 1996), n.p.

11. U.S. Department of Health and Human Services, "Child Mistreatment 1998: Reports From the States to the National Child Abuse and Neglect Data System," *Administration on Children, Youth and Families,* 2000. http://www.calib.com/nccanch/stats/index.cfm#ncands (accessed August 25, 2003).

12. U.S. Department of Health and Human Services, Children's Bureau, "National Child Abuse and Neglect Data System. Summary of Key Findings From Calendar Year 2000," *Caliber Associates,* April 2002. http://www.calib.com/nccanch/stats/index.cfm#ncands (accessed August 25, 2003).

13. U.S. Department of Justice, *Office of Juvenile Justice and Delinquency Prevention.* http://ojjdp.ncjrs.org/ (accessed August 23, 2003).

14. U.S. Department of Health and Human Services, Children's Bureau, "National Child Abuse and Neglect Data System. Summary of Key Findings From Calendar Year 2000."

15. *Chicago Tribune,* December 14, 1992, n.p.

16. *Post Standard* (Syracuse, NY), October 25, 1994, n.p.

17. Stephen Naysmith, "Alarming Increase in Number of Girl Bullies," *The Sunday Herald,* May 5, 2002, p. 10. http://www.sundayherald.com/ (accessed August 27, 2003).

18. Kate Moody, *Growing Up on Television, (*New York: McGraw-Hill, 1984), n.p.

19. Packard, *Our Endangered Children,* p. 98.

20. Roger Thompson, "Kids Rule," *Preaching Today* (May 1996), audiocassette (Carol Stream, IL: Christianity Today, May 1996), sermon 152.

21. Robert Coles, quoted in Roger Thompson, "Kids Rule," *Preaching Today* (May 1996), audiocassette (Carol Stream, IL: Christianity Today, May 1996), sermon 152.

22. Source unknown.

23. Packard, *Our Endangered Children,* p. 28.

Chapter 3

1. Vincent Ryan Ruggiero, *Warning: Nonsense Is Destroying America* (Nashville, TN: Thomas Nelson Publishers, 1994), p. 51.

2. Garrison Keillor, quoted in Debra K. Klingsporn and Anne Buchanan, comps., *One Hundred Voices* (Bloomington, MN: Front Porch Books, 1999), p. 120.

3. C. S. Lewis, quoted in Rayn Ruggiero, *Warning: Nonsense Is Destroying America* (Nashville, TN: Thomas Nelson Publishers, 1994), p. 21.

4. Benjamin Franklin, quoted in Ted Goodman, ed., *The Forbes Book of Business Quotations* (New York: Black Dog and Leventhal Publishers, 1997), p. 840.

5. Cal Thomas, *USA Today,* March 29, 1996, n.p.

6. El-Khawasa, "Campus Trends 1995," (Washington, D.C.: American Council on Education, 1995), n.p.

7. John Steinbeck, quoted in Os Guiness, *The American Hour* (New York: Freedom Press, 1993), p. 306.

8. Os Guiness, *The American Hour* (New York: Freedom Press, 1993), p. 305.

9. Robert Finch, quoted in Carolyn R. Shaffer and Kristin Anundsen, *Creating Community Anywhere* (New York: Putnam Publishing Group, 1993), p. 95.

10. Lee Salk, *Familyhood* (New York: Simon and Schuster, 1992), p. 26.

11. Charles Sell, *Family Ministry* (Grand Rapids, MI: Zondervan Publishing House, 1995), p. 28.

12. Angela Elwell Hunt, "What Children of Divorce Really Think," *Christian Reader,* May/June 1997. http://www.christianitytoday.com (accessed August 25, 2003).

13. George Bernard Shaw, quoted in Charles Handy, *The Age of Paradox* (Boston: Harvard Business School Press, 1995), p. 279.

Chapter 4

1. Source unknown.

2. David Gergen, "Keeping Faith in Kids," *U.S. News and World Report* (May 31, 1999), p. 80.

3. Ibid.

4. Elton Trueblood, *The Incendiary Fellowship* (New York: Harper and Row Publishers, 1967), p. 71.

5. William Raspberry, "Politicians Can't Fix Our Problems—But We Can," *Gazette Telegraph* (Colorado Springs, CO), April 23, 1996, Commentary Section D-3.

6. George Barna, quoted in Rob Wilkins, "Reinventing the Church," *Life and Work,* vol. 2, no. 2 (March/April 1999), n.p.

7. Ibid.

8. Barbara Brown Taylor, "True Purpose," *Christian Century* (February 21, 2001), p. 30.

9. Ibid.

10. Tony Campolo, *Wake Up America!: Answering God's Radical Call While Living in the Real World* (New York: HarperCollins Publishers, 1991), p. 146.

11. Ibid., p. 148.

12. Kathleen Parker, "Protests in Poor Taste," *Denver Post,* May 1, 1999, sec. B, p. 7.

13. John Updike, quoted in Rebecca Davis and Susan Mesner, eds., *The Treasury of Religious and Spiritual Quotations: Words to Live By* (Pleasantville, NY: Reader's Digest, 1994), p. 81.

14. Tony Campolo, quoted in Rebecca Davis and Susan Mesner, eds., *The Treasury of Religious and Spiritual Quotations: Words to Live By* (Pleasantville, NY: Reader's Digest, 1994), pp. 152-153.

15. Rebecca Davis and Susan Mesner, eds., *The Treasury of Religious and Spiritual Quotations: Words to Live By* (Pleasantville, NY: Reader's Digest, 1994), p. 179.

16. Rick Ezell, *Strengthening the Pastor's Soul* (Grand Rapids, MI: Kregel Publications, 2003), n.p.

Chapter 5

1. Vance Packard, *Our Endangered Children: Growing Up in a Changing World* (Boston: Little, Brown and Company, 1983), p. 26.

2. Rosemary Harris, *Gazette Telegraph* (Colorado Springs, CO), April 12, 1996, n.p.

3. *Merriam-Webster's Collegiate Dictionary*, 10th ed., s.v. "ombudsman."

4. Dr. Virginia Patterson (speech presented at the Helping Children Follow Jesus Conference, Wheaton Graduate School, Wheaton, IL, n.d.).

5. *Gazette Telegraph* (Colorado Springs, CO), April 8, 1996, n.p.

6. Ibid.

7. Lee Salk, *Familyhood* (New York: Simon and Schuster, 1992), p. 191.

8. Source unknown.

Chapter 6

1. T. Crichton Mitchell, quoted in H. Ray Dunning and Neil B. Wiseman, eds., *Biblical Resources for Holiness Preaching* (Kansas City, MO: Beacon Hill Press, 1990), p. 54.

2. Richard D. Dobbins, *The Family-Friendly Church* (Altamonte Springs, FL: Creation House, 1989), p. 12.

3. Lee Salk, *Familyhood* (New York: Simon and Schuster, 1992), p. 19.

4. James Dobson, "Keys to a Family-Friendly Church," *Leadership* (winter 1986), p. 16.

5. Richard P. Olson and Joe H. Leonard, Jr., *A New Day for Family Ministry* (New York: The Alban Institute, 1996), p. 82.

6. Rodney Clapp, quoted in Charles M. Sell, *Family Ministry* (Grand Rapids, MI: Zondervan Publishing House, 1995), p. 71.

7. Charles M. Sell, *Family Ministry* (Grand Rapids, MI: Zondervan Publishing House, 1995), p. 74.

8. Paul Caminiti, "How Many Meetings Do We Need?" *Leadership* (winter 1986), p. 123.

9. Michael S. Lawson and Robert J. Choun, Jr., *Directing Christian Education* (Chicago: Moody Press, 1992), p. 24.

10. Jack O. Balswick and Judith K. Balswick, *The Family: A Christian Perspective on the Contemporary Home* (Grand Rapids, MI: Baker Book House, 1999), p. 306.

11. Tex Sample, *Hard Living People and Mainstream Christians* (Nashville, TN: Abingdon Press, 1993), n.p.

Chapter 7

1. Paul Pearsall, *Power of the Family* (New York: Bantam Dell Publishing Group, 1990), p. 4.

2. Robert Frost, "The Death of a Hired Man," *North of Boston: Poems* (New York: Dodd, Mead, 1977).

3. Halford Luccock, *The Acts of the Apostles* (New York: Willett, Clark and Company, 1938), pp. 28-29.

4. Louis Pasteur, quoted in Linda Mintle, *Kids Killing Kids* (Lake Mary, FL: Creation House, 1999), p. 28.

5. Amy Carmichael, *Christian Globe*. http://www.christianglobe.com/ Illustrations/theDetails.asp?whichOne=c&whichFile=children (accessed August 28, 2003).

6. Edmund Burke, "Letter to a Member of the National Assembly," *The Works of the Right Honorable Edmund Burke*, quoted in Frances Hesselbein, *Community of the Future* (San Francisco: Jossey-Bass, 1998), p. 69.

7. Richard Lischer, *The Preacher King* (New York: Oxford Press, 1995), p. 22.

Chapter 8

1. Charles M. Sell, *Family Ministry* (Grand Rapids, MI: Zondervan Publishing House, 1981), p. 259.

2. Source unknown.

3. Os Guiness, *The American Hour* (Monroe, LA: Free Press, 1994), p. 306.

4. Wavelyn Beltz Dreher, "God Called (with a Little Help)," 1996. Used by permission.

5. Dr. Miriam Hall, speech presented on June 27, 1993.

6. Ibid.

Chapter 9

1. Robert Coles, *The Call of Service* (Boston: Houghton Mifflin Company, 1993), p. 69.

2. Jerry Bock, *Fiddler on the Roof,* quoted in, Carol Van Klompenburg, "The Value of Traditions in the Family," *Current Thoughts and Trends* (February 1996), p. 12.

Chapter 10

1. Charles M. Sell, *Family Ministry* (Grand Rapids, MI: Zondervan Publishing House, 1995), p. 157.
2. Les and Leslie Parrott, "Today's Family: Holding Tough in Tough Times," *Holiness Today* (March 2003), p. 15.
3. Ibid.
4. U.S. Department of Health and Human Services, "Promoting Responsible Fatherhood," *U.S. Department of Health and Human Services,* April 26, 2002, http://www.fatherhood.hhs.gov, p. 1.
5. U.S. Bureau of Census, "America's Families and Living Arrangements," *Current Population Reports,* March 2000. http://www.census.gov/popula tion/www/socdemo/hh-fam.html (accessed August 25, 2003), quoted in "What Does a Family Look Like Today?" *Holiness Today* (March 2003), p. 30.
6. Linda J. Waite and Maggie Gallagher, *The Case for Marriage* (New York: Doubleday, 2000).
7. Maggie Gallagher, "Why Marriage Is Good for You," *City Journal of Manhattan,* vol. 10, no. 4 (Autumn 2000), http://www.city-journal.org/ html/10_4_why_marriage_is.html (accessed August 28, 2003).
8. Ibid.
9. Ibid.
10. Wayne Martindale and Jerry Root, ed., *The Quotable Lewis* (Wheaton, IL: Tyndale, 1963), p. 419.
11. Barna Research Group, "Family in America," *Barna Research Online,* February 1992. http://www.barna.org/cgi-bin/home.asp (accessed August 25, 2003).
12. *Bartlett's Familiar Quotations* (Boston: Little, Brown and Company, 1980), p. 138.
13. Dr. Richard Kremler, quoted in Charles E. Blair, *The Silent Thousands Speak* (Grand Rapids, MI: Zondervan Publishing House, 1968), p. 54.
14. Charles E. Blair, *The Silent Thousands Speak* (Grand Rapids, MI: Zondervan Publishing House, 1968), p. 82.
15. Sell, *Family Ministry,* p. 157.

Chapter 11

1. John Baillie, quoted in Debra K. Klingsporn and Anne Buchanan, comps., *One Hundred Voices* (Bloomington, MN: Front Porch Books, 1999), p. 66.

2. Miles McPherson and Wayne Rice, "Replace Meetings with Mentors," *Youthworker* (fall 1995), p. 28.

3. *Gazette Telegraph* (Colorado Springs, CO), April 9, 1996, n.p.

4. Richard D. Dobbins, *The Family-Friendly Church* (Altamonte Springs, FL: Creation House, 1989), p. 97.

5. Samuel L. Hamilton, *Religion in Life* (summer 1949), p. 18.

6. Jeanette Lauer and Robert Lauer, quoted in Richard P. Olson and Joe H. Leonard, Jr., *A New Day for Family Ministry* (New York: The Alban Institute, 1996), p. 94.

7. Charles Swindoll, *Living on the Ragged Edge* (Waco, TX: Word Books, 1985), p. 11, quoted in Charles M. Sell, *Family Ministry* (Grand Rapids, MI: Zondervan Publishing House, 1995), p. 177.

8. George Whitefield, quoted in Charles M. Sell, *Family Ministry* (Grand Rapids, MI: Zondervan Publishing House, 1995), p. 178.

9. Charles M. Sell, *Family Ministry* (Grand Rapids, MI: Zondervan Publishing House, 1995), p. 324.

10. Ibid., p. 356.

11. "Family in America," *Journal of Youth and Adolescence* (February 1996), quoted in "Haste vs. Chaste," *Current Thoughts and Trends* (April 1996), p. 10.

Also from H. B. London, Jr., and Neil B. Wiseman

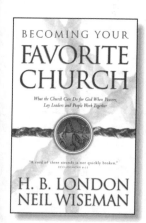

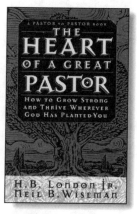

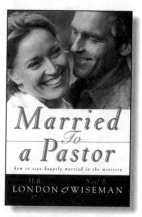

Becoming Your Favorite Church
What the Church Can Do for God When Pastors, Lay Leaders and People Work Together
Paperback • ISBN 08307.29046

The Heart of a Great Pastor
How to Grow Strong and Thrive Wherever God Has Planted You
Paperback • ISBN 08307.16890

Married to a Pastor
How to Stay Happily Married in the Ministry
Paperback • ISBN 08307.25059

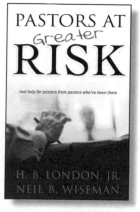

They Call Me Pastor
How to Love the Ones You Lead
Paperback • ISBN 08307.23900

Pastors at Greater Risk
Real Help for Pastors from Pastors Who Have Been There
Hardcover • ISBN 08307.29038